LEAD POISONING

To John Stevens —

Nothing lasts like an old friend —

1991

To the one person without whom
this book could not have been
written: the little asshole that shot me.

LEAD POISONING

POISONING

25 TRUE STORIES FROM THE WRONG END OF A GUN

CHRIS PFOUTS

PALADIN PRESS
BOULDER, COLORADO

Lead Poisoning:
25 True Stories from the Wrong End of a Gun
by Chris Pfouts

Copyright © 1991 by John Christopher Pfouts

ISBN 0-87364-620-7
Printed in the United States of America

Library of Congress Catalog Number: 90-53682

Published by Paladin Press, a division of
Paladin Enterprises, Inc., P.O. Box 1307,
Boulder, Colorado 80306, USA.
(303) 443-7250

Direct inquires and/or orders to the above address.

■ CONTENTS

Introduction ■ 1

A Note About Interviewing ■ 16

Dan ■ 18

Michael ■ 26

Frank ■ 30

Travis Beck ■ 40

Randy Walker ■ 43

Dragon ■ 58

Joe Wentz ■ 64

Jimmy the Greek ■ 67

Roland ■ 71

Laura Newman ■ 79

"New York" ■ 83

Detective Sergeant Martin Barrett ■ 92

Steve Fuller ■ 96

Roger Kane ■ 101

Big Daddy ■ 106

Dean R. Kahler ■ 113

Dum Dum ■ 121

Pat Delehanty ■ 129

Frankie L. ■ 133

Steve Malinchoc ■ 142

Horacio ■ 145

Crazy Ace ■ 154

Harley Swiftdeer ■ 156

Preston Townes ■ 170

■ ACKNOWLEDGMENTS

No research work is done in a vacuum. As I put this book together, I found a lot of people who were willing to aid and abet, and their help was invaluable. They were: my parents, Ray August, Jack Quigley, Big Dennis, Roger Bloomfield, Janice Marie Johnson, Marc MacYoung, Brett Botula, Joe Ranker, Shotsie Gorman, Jack Dempsey, Whipps, Robert Sager, Garfield, Gregory Fleeman, Marty Weidenbaum, Jim Travers, Jamie Kitman, Jon Ford, and the Lindsay family—Big Nick, Little Nick, Frances, Edward, David, Karen. And, of course, everyone who took the time to talk with me.

■ INTRODUCTION

"Something is desperately wrong for I feel
A deep burning pain in my side . . ."
                              —Marty Robbins, "El Paso"

Bullets are like Hallmark Cards: you get one when somebody cares enough to send the very best. I got my bullet, I hope my only bullet, on a dark street corner in Brooklyn. This book was really born the second that guy pulled the .38 out from under his jacket, because in that instant life stopped being what it had been before and turned into a river of urgent questions: Am I gonna live through this? Could I really be bleeding to death? Will I ever walk again?

In time, most of the questions answered themselves. I didn't bleed to death because EMS got there fast enough; inside of fifteen minutes I was pretty sure that wouldn't happen. A couple days passed before I knew I was going to live, but by then the pain was so bad I didn't know if I wanted to. When it came to walking, the doctors allowed that I would. How well, they wouldn't say. That question dragged on unanswered for many months.

Between all the operations and injections and IVs, the hospital sent a couple shrinks around to my bed. I honestly don't remember if they were psychologists or counselors or what. It didn't matter that much anyway. I learned to mistrust and dislike headshrinkers when I was a juvenile delinquent, and nothing I've heard or read or been through since has altered that opinion. I would have talked to them, though, if they had correctly answered one simple question: Have you ever been shot?

They hadn't, and there was nothing further for us to talk about. You don't have to be a leper to treat lepers, I know that, but I wasn't going to lie there and spill my guts to somebody who had never been through anything more traumatic than a blind date. It would have been worse than a waste of time.

When I got back on the streets I found what I was looking for—guys who'd survived lead poisoning. I sat them down and listened to their stories, told mine, and started getting better. It was that simple.

I brought a tape recorder along from the beginning. In the hospital I realized that a book of survivors' stories would be more valuable to a gunshot victim than all the Jung and Freud in China. Theories don't mean a thing in the wake of a bullet, and real information on how to survive a shooting was just not available. Believe me, there's a lot to know.

That was my original aim, to give recovered gunshot victims a chance to talk to others who weren't so far along. It would have helped me; I figured it would help others. If you look hard enough for an answer you will eventually find just the right one. Roger Kane, one of the men in this book, had injuries similar to mine but much more severe in some aspects. Today he's completely jake. You look at him and you'd never know that once upon a time Roger Kane was lying on the ground with his body parts in such complete disarray that he thought he was a crowd. If Roger Kane—or anybody that had been hit bad in a way similar to how I was hit—had come into my hospital room and done a few quick calisthenics, it would have dissolved most of my stress and worry. I would have known *from somebody who had been there* that you could heal up after a bullet and get on with your life.

In the beginning, pain colored everything. I felt then that this book would turn out to be a polemic against the hurt and grief that guns can cause. That wasn't necessarily what I wanted, but it looked like the direction the material wanted to go. The important thing was to get the stories between covers. I've been around guns all my life. My father was an avid hunter for many years and a dead-on skeet shooter. I'm less of a sportsman and more of a hood, but I've owned dozens of guns, all kinds. I like guns, and getting shot didn't change that. But for this book, my opinion wasn't important. If getting shot was all about pain, then so be it.

I'm happy to say that my assessment of these stories has come around 180 degrees since the beginning. I'm not freighted with constant pain anymore, and I see a little clearer. These stories are not just about pain, they're about survival, triumph, life. You can learn about staying alive from this book. Several of these people died and came back. There is nothing mystical or otherworldly about it. They got shot dead, passed over, and returned to tell the tale. It puzzles the doctors and it puzzles the survivors. When I was dying it puzzled me.

I believe that a lot of people die from gunshot wounds because they expect to die. Other people live after the docs are ready to drop them into the long box. Who knows why? The basic fact is that a bullet is the wildest Hallmark Card of all, a radical ace. Once the lead goes in, nobody knows anything for sure.

There aren't even any statistics worth wiping your ass with. The U.S. Department of Justice released a study in mid-1990 claiming that about 15,000 people are nonfatally shot *with pistols* in an average year. Gun-control groups say that between 40,000 and 70,000 people are nonfatally shot in the U.S. every year. Thirty thousand give or take is a mighty wide gray area.

Behind the stats are stories, of course. There were a few people I wanted to interview but couldn't. The one that really sticks out was a cop in northern New Jersey. He had stopped a car on the highway and been shot in the ballistic vest. I thought that a happy-ending story like that would be a great way to cap off the book. Bonehead, a friend of mine, had known the cop since they were kids.

The cop agreed to talk to me, but we couldn't quite hook up. Then he balked, and Bonehead had a hard time finding him. Finally he just vanished. Then one night I turned on the TV and there was my cop, in a mental institution called Bergen Pines. He had checked himself in a few hours before, and his department was alleging that he had staged not only the vest incident, in which he allegedly shot himself, but also an earlier stabbing incident and a chase in which his patrol car had been shot up. Why would a guy do this? Promotion? Attention? Maybe he just saw too many John Wayne movies. I had a little bit of the John Wayne problem myself until I got shot.

It was March 6, 1988; cold, but not the bitter heart of winter. The snow that still remained was dirty, hard, and old. It was an hour into Sunday morning, and Bedford Avenue was popping with activity. Williamsburg is one of Brooklyn's worst neighborhoods, and this block was one of Williamsburg's worst. That's saying something. It looked like the Mutant's Midway: crack, junk, coke all the time *amigo*, whores, lepers, zombies, the living soon-to-be-dead with Kaposi's sarcoma dotted all over their faces. My name is Lesion. Unlike the cops, the werewolves were everywhere, circling, chanting singsong about their dope, *Gold top, man, the Unknown, we got DOA man*, brand name crack and junk, selling, scoring, half visible in the darkness.

It was my street. I'd had a great apartment for a month. Despite my block, and a few others like it, Williamsburg was coming up quickly. Only one stop out of Manhattan on either of two subway lines, and less than five minutes from the East Village by car or motorcycle, it was fast transforming into another yuppie paradise. I'm no yuppie, just a guy looking for a decent place to live. My apartment was a full floor, completely renovated, with two working fireplaces and a bathroom that was a labor of love by a man who understood bathrooms. More important, it was cheap. Just a little annoyance on the street coming and going, no sweat. On the rare occasions when the street action bothered me, I looked at the ceiling fan, the new kitchen, the quality Sheetrock, and forgot about it. For the first time in ten years I wasn't living in a shithole. When I gave the landlord money I didn't feel like the joke was on me.

I had a hot date coming over that night and she was running late. Kelly's never been on time for anything in her life. I'd spent a couple hours spiffing the place up, and I wanted to take out the garbage and grab a six-pack at the corner before she showed. It was such a casual, routine trip that I slid bare feet into motorcycle boots and threw a heavy down parka over an undershirt. I made sure the door was latched tight behind me when I stepped into the street. I crossed the avenue, then the street at the corner, and winged the trash bag underhand into a garbage can.

"Get that shit out of there," a man said from the shadows. "Thass my can."

"Go fuck yourself," I said. Who's got time for some asshole who thinks he owns a trash can? I recrossed Bedford Avenue to the bodega for my beer.

At that time of night you do your bodega business through a thick plexiglass lazy Susan in the front window. It's a high-crime area. People were lined up on the sidewalk and I got in line. The king of the trash can followed me across the avenue carrying my trash bag and threw it at my feet.

That's when I realized I was dealing with two guys, the trash tyrant and a quiet sidekick. Now it was a fight coming for sure, a fight I expected to lose. I've never beaten two guys in my life. One thing was sure, I couldn't run. Couldn't take any lip and couldn't run. Being white made me part of a small local minority, and being big just made me more obvious. I was a gentrifier with a nine hundred dollar a month apartment (and a roommate) in a food-stamp neighborhood. More than anything else I was new on the block, and like new fish everywhere I had to have my balls weighed. If I picked up the trash bag and hopped to this little asshole's orders, I'd never have another minute of peace.

So they might as well get used to my living there. At that point, the outcome of the fight didn't matter that much. The question was if I would stand or run. At least that's how I saw it. That's how Shane would have seen it. I moved back a step or two to get the bodega wall closer to my unprotected spine.

The Hefty bag lay between us on the dirty Brooklyn cement. I could hear cat litter shifting inside like fat sand in a giant egg timer. It got that quiet. I looked the main man in the face, seeing rampant crack for the first time. It's like a ghostly electricity, squirming flat and opaque in the pupils. "So you did that." I nodded at the bag. "Now whattaya gonna do?"

"I'm gonna do this, motherfucker," he said. He tugged the revolver out of his waistband and shot me.

I went down, not sure for a moment where I'd been hit. Maybe I could have run and there wasn't quite time, or maybe I really did turn to run and that's why the bullet entered at the angle it did. Possibly I just stood there gawking like a hayseed at a sideshow. I really don't know. There was a scratch of time when he first put his hand on the pistol grip that I thought it must be a toy. Sort of like prayed it was a toy, though I'm not a praying man. And at the same time I knew it wasn't. It's pathetic as hell to Barnum yourself in an emergency. Worse, it doesn't work.

By the time he fired I knew damn good and well that it was a real gun, and my big worry was where he was going to give it to me. Gut or head, I thought I'd be dead right there. I'd read that being gut-shot hurts like hell. I thought I'd die in pain—but that was before I had a real thorough understanding of the horizonless seas of red agony a human can fall into. The term "kneecapping," even when I was down and looking at a big bullet hole just above my own right kneecap, didn't occur to me.

The sound of the gunshot was distant, almost muffled. I remember wondering why I could hear it at all; nobody in war movies hears the one with his name on it. I'll tell you, though, you get shot on a Brooklyn street corner and you hear it.

At its wimpiest and slowest, a .38 Special revolver with a 6-inch barrel—the gun I was shot with—has a muzzle velocity of 850 feet per second. At peak power the same pistol can deliver lead at over 1,200 fps. No matter what the load, less than a hundredth of a second went by between trigger pull and thigh trauma. We were only about six feet apart.

I landed on the sidewalk, back against the bodega. It took a second or so before the blood began to come from the neat little hole, and then it flowed freely, warm and red. I squeezed my thigh with both hands.

The pistol was still pointed at me, then it lowered, dropped, and finally went away. Just went away and left me alone. When I was sure he wasn't going to shoot me anymore, I just sat and felt it. Blood soaked my jeans and dripped onto the sidewalk. Thoughts flew like cards in a game of 52 pickup. It seemed there were people around, like tourists in the bleachers watching a bull die on the arena sands. My arena was filthy concrete surrounded by buildings full of poverty. There were no crisp trumpets and no cheers.

I didn't want to die there.

I held my leg and struggled upright while trying to stanch the wound. My building was halfway down the block, and I staggered toward it.

More than pain or fear or bleeding, all of which there was in abundance, my biggest enemy was shock. Shock will kill you with kindness. You feel it coming on, warm and inviting and insidious, like waves of soft, welcome Valium easing in. Shock wants you to be comfortable and relax. Shock wants to take your mind off all that nasty pain. I had insane thoughts as I limped along: *I'd have to get a sidecar for my motorcycle now. Was that raindrops or pigeon shit or was I bleeding up? My best jeans were ruined. Harry O the TV detective lived in Venice Beach.*

Worse than the lunatic distractions, shock wanted me to sit right back down on the sidewalk and take a load off the old dogs. The urge to settle comfortably into a snowbank and bleed quietly was nearly overpowering. It would be so soft and easy. Moving along was so hard.

Already my foot felt cold, and it was no trick of shock. My right foot was in deep trouble and I knew it. Later, in the hospital, I told everyone who came close that my foot was graveyard cold. That was the word that came to mind as I dragged along the sidewalk: graveyard cold. I was sure I would lose it.

At the door of my building a jungle of tangled shock confusion fought me as I looked for the right key. It was almost my Waterloo right there. Thoughts cascaded down on each other and I lost track of what I was doing. There was a Martha and the Vandellas record on the turntable; who will put it back in the sleeve? I should make a dental appointment. These bricks need new paint.

No. Keys. Find the key, the one with the big square head. Eventually I did, opening the door and lurching along the hall to the staircase. I have no idea how I climbed that single flight, but somehow it happened and after a smaller version of the battle at the front door, I found the apartment key and got in. Behind me, from all the blood, the hall and staircase looked like the climactic scene from *Taxi Driver*. I was pretty well sure I was dying by then, and I have a clear recollection of looking at my right hand, which was thickly wet with my own fresh blood, and purposely slapping a big red handprint on the white wall. "Charlie Manson," came the thought, and for a second I seriously considered writing "pigs" above the handprint. One last joke. Always leave 'em laughing. Only it was too hard to do.

I virtually fell into the apartment, leaving the door open. I moved to sit in a chair, but I was so weak already that I knew I'd have to go down to the floor later. Why waste time. Eliminate the middleman. My right boot was full of blood and I yanked it off. A boot full of blood is something you read about in Civil War novels and not something you expect to actually wear. It's scary how much blood a size eleven motorcycle boot will hold. I got the other boot off, too, threw my bloody coat aside, and got on the floor with the cordless phone. The phone was a new toy, a gift. I can't recommend them enough for those trying times when you're lying in a widening pool of your own blood and making calls.

Even while I was pushing the three phone buttons, shock was wondering if I should bring a book in case there was a long line at the hospital. 911 picked up on the second ring. I told them in my clearest, calmest voice that I'd just been shot and I thought I was bleeding to death. My foot is cold. Please send someone to help and soon. I knew my address and told them what it was. Then I phoned a friend of mine. His was the only other number I could remember just then and he doesn't usually go out on Saturday nights. When he picked up I explained fast and blunt and told him to please call 911 and double my request for help—which was also insurance in case I had hallucinated the first call—and then phone me back until help showed or I died, whichever came first.

We were talking when EMS and the cops arrived.

Insectlike, tinny voices came through the intercom speaker from the street below: Was I hurt? Were they in the right place? At the time it didn't occur to me, but there must have been a good splash of blood outside the door.

The questions seemed to come for a long time. I didn't have the strength to get up and push the little white button and tell them to bust the damn door in and hurry. My foot is so cold . . . the phone fell out past the end of my arm, gone. I whispered at the ceiling. It was all I could do. The questions continued and I was unable to reply. It looked like I was going to die after all, with help only a few feet away.

When they did finally break in I let go completely and allowed myself to float away, across the Styx if that's what was supposed to happen. I was in total, indescribable peace, dying, serene beyond the reckoning of the living. At last, finally, I was above strife and turmoil. Peace is sweeter and calmer than I ever could have imagined and I welcomed it, opened myself up to join it. I had done everything I could do to save myself and now it was up to the cops and the medics. I was at one with the universe.

Somehow they hauled me back from the peace of dying. My date, Kelly, arrived to see them carry me out the front door and load me into the meat wagon.

Everything was warm compared to my foot. We must be in for an early spring, I thought. Might be good bass fishing this year (I hadn't been fishing for bass or anything else in ten years). They left me in the back of the ambulance with the doors open and I looked out into the cold street. Kelly climbed in looking scared and kissed me. I gave her the keys to the house and told her to make sure it was locked and to chase any residual cops out.

Potholes do not spare ambulances. Strapped into my gurney, I bounced around the back of that bus like a ball. If I screamed at any point during the night, it was in the meat wagon.

The cold in my foot was no illusion. The bullet had severed the femoral artery and shut off the blood to my lower leg. It also broke my femur, taking an inch-wide bite out of the bone without breaking it in two. In the emergency room, chaos reigned. A medico made me choke and puke, and threatened to jam tubes down my throat if I didn't puke right. A doctor working on me yelled, "Does this patient have an exit wound?" Another yelled, "Is this patient hypertensive?" Me, high blood pressure? Mister, I got a leak in my system a mile wide. No pressure at all.

Sometime before surgery my gurney was pushed into a room full of empty gurneys. There was nothing else in there but me and the carts. It looked like a storage room. They left me alone and it was terrifying. I heard someone say that a kid had come in with a "big caliber in the lower right quadrant." I knew what that meant, hole in the gut, bad news. Bad news for me, too, maybe worse than for the vic. I was alone in a storage room with a graveyard foot, about to die, because they had to triage that kid ahead of me. I was going to die on the domino plan. Look at all the ways a total stranger can kill you. I no longer had the strength to even whisper.

When I woke up in the ICU, which is the next thing I remember, I got a good fat shot of Demerol the instant my eyelids fluttered up. Disoriented, scared, hurting bad, a double slurpee injection is just what you need. I really came to treasure those shots. And even though they kept me whacked out to Alpha Centauri with that dope, there were dressing changes on the wound—twice daily demonstrations of how acute pain can cut through anything in the pharmacopeia.

Under the bandages my leg was a waxy, dead thing. The bullet hole was as neat as if it had been drilled into wood. On the inside of my thigh and on both sides of the calf were long slashes where the skin was peeled back. At the edges of these wounds the flesh looked pickled, and the dark orange hospital disinfectant made the color appear even more malignant. Huge raw steaks bulged out of these slashes.

The steaks were my muscles. The slashes go by the medical name fasciotomies, and surgeons perform this operation to offset compartment syndrome. When blood flow to muscles is interrupted for a long period and then the plumbing is hooked back up, muscles swell up like balloons. The fasciotomies give them room to swell freely. My exposed, distended muscles were a leaden red color, and if I hadn't been mostly unconscious anyway, I would have fainted just from looking at them.

Changing the dressings involved stripping off the bandages, removing the packings from around the exposed muscles, and tugging the gauze plug out of the bullet hole. This last bit, no matter how gently it was done, hurt like they were ripping my dick off. Packing the gauze back in later hurt worse. Once the whole leg was exposed, they scrubbed it all down with saline solution, poured saline into the bullet hole, and wrapped it all up again.

Woodhull Hospital is a wing of Hell, and I say that with the full awareness that their ER doctors saved my leg and my life. It is a public hospital and it treats the public, which is always a problem. The public is more of a problem in that part of Brooklyn than it is in most places. Many of the citizens treated at Woodhull are injured prisoners who require a cop on hand at all times. There were many cops on my floor. There were many patients. But there were damned few nurses. Once I waited six hours for a pain shot that was due every three hours and mercilessly overdue at three hours and one minute. When it finally arrived its bearer was a snarling Jamaican virago who cursed me loud and long for my selfishness—other people were suffering needlessly because I wanted my three-hour shot every six hours. Another time I asked an aide for a bedpan pronto and she told me they didn't have any more. I told her to stand by for a hell of a mess. She did finally locate one, but it took an hour.

There was a patient down the hall who screamed all day and night for a nurse that I'm sure never came. I understood. I felt sorry for the guy. I solved my attention-getting problem through another patient, a daffy old man they called Poppy. Poppy was hooked up to a whole forest of IV trees. He hated bedpans and liked to pee in the bathroom, but when he stood up, down came the IVs, smash. He couldn't walk, either. He'd just stand up and fall over. When they strapped him down he undid the straps. There was another guy in the room, but he was hooked up to an aquarium and could barely talk. The head nurse came to me and asked if I'd call out when Poppy started making his move for the bathroom. I told her I would if they'd come when I called and if she promised to keep the dope close to schedule. So we worked that out.

It sounds like a joke to complain about the food, but yellow ham is never funny and Woodhull's chow was so bad, no exaggeration, that after leaving the ICU and not having eaten for five days running, I still couldn't choke the stuff down. I was afraid of it. The roaches liked it, though, and they were everywhere. My bedside table had dozens living in it.

Maybe worst of all is the absence of patient phones. It scares the bejesus out of people far away when they hear you've been shot and gone critical and they can't reach you by phone. And people in Woodhull want ice water, too.

I transferred out of there as fast as I could, which saved my life just as sure as phoning 911 did. But before I left I got a booklet from the New York State Crime Victims Board. It explained that monetary compensation is available to victims of violent crime. I could cash in.

My new home was Cabrini Medical Center in Manhattan. Here was sanity, compassion, a full staff, and decent food. Great food, in fact. Better food than I eat at home. In less than a month I was out with a full leg cast covering a bone pin, bone graft, and three large skin grafts.

From the beginning it was obvious that the cops were never even going to get a whiff of the guy that shot me. I wasn't much help. That whole neighborhood is Puerto Rican, and he looked and sounded Puerto Rican. The muzzle of his revolver was round with a sight blade on top. And that was all I could tell them.

Nobody on the street was talking, which didn't surprise me. Some of my friends went out and tried to bribe a name out of some local junkies, but they wouldn't give. The guy was a seasoned pro, there's no doubt about that. His fast draw, lack of hesitation or nervousness, and choice of the kneecap as a target all indicate that I was just one more nick in a very notched grip. Among deer hunters there's a famous disease called Buck Fever that causes overexcited hunters to prematurely jerk-fire their rifles in any direction the deer isn't. Some duck hunters crap in their waders over a few incoming mallards and fill empty sky with wasted shot while the ducks veer off to safety. Amateurs panic, and amateurs waste shots. My guy was cool and calm with his pistol, loose and relaxed. The two-bit street corner version of Al Pacino's Tony Montana in *Scarface*. No wonder the local Puerto Ricans didn't want to snitch on this guy, even for a price. They didn't want to rat themselves into a bed in Woodhull. Or worse.

Not that the cops were doing such a hotshot investigation anyway. Two detectives appeared at the foot of my bed in

Woodhull, an alcoholic-looking middle-aged white man and a young black woman. They introduced themselves and launched right into the clumsiest good cop/bad cop routine I ever heard. I couldn't quite believe it.

"You better tell us who shotcha, pal," the alky rasped. His hands were jammed deep in his sport coat pockets and he looked like he needed a drink bad.

"Don't be so rough on him, come on." The woman's voice was warm and sympathetic. "Can't you see he's in pain?"

"He's lucky he isn't in Hell. Just give us the name and we'll go from there, sonny. Who shotcha?"

"Take it easy, now. Mr. Pfouts, would you recognize him if you saw him again?"

"He knows, he just ain't talking."

The woman detective gave me her card, but it was actually another detective's card, she explained. She scribbled out the old name and wrote hers in. When I phoned her a month later to check on things, another detective, a man, told me she was off the force temporarily. In fact, he had my case, yes, right there in the pile. I wrote his name on the card. When I called again in one more month, that guy was gone and yet another detective had the case. No, no word yet. I added his name to the list on the card. About six months after I got shot I threw the card away. It had five names on it.

It's been two and a half years now. Because of nerve damage I got drop foot and cannot raise my right foot to more than 90 degrees. Drop foot makes you trip all the time, which is an enormous pain in the ass. Slowly the nerves are regenerating, though, and I have more range of movement now than I did six months ago.

There are other lasting effects. I quit smoking the night I got shot, gave up twenty years of cigarettes with a bullet. Nothing short of forced abstention on deep narcotics or being marooned on Gilligan's Island could have done it.

And there is this book. If you've been shot, you'll feel right at home. These are your people. If you haven't been shot, you can learn a great deal from what these people have to say. Everyone is at risk for lead poisoning in this world; it's a fact of life. You can learn to survive and heal. You can learn to avoid the bullet in the first place.

In the process of putting this work together I've answered most of the questions that started when that guy pulled his gun. Now my questions are about how to enjoy life more and make the best use of my time. Those are the only goals that seem worth pursuing.

New York City, 1990

■ A Note About Interviewing

"And though he tread the humble ways of men
He shall not speak the common tongue again."
—Mary Brent Whiteside

There are twenty-five people in this book who have been shot, including myself. My story is in the Introduction. Dum Dum, who is a talented writer, also authored his own piece. All the rest are taken from taped interviews without being slicked up, restructured, or polished. When I talk to people, I let them tell their story in their own way. I never try to direct a story or slew it off its course. Questions were only asked for clarification or amplification.

I talked to these people in diners, bars, offices, studios, and in a few cases, over the phone. I dislike the telephone for this kind of work, but sometimes it just wasn't practical to travel as far as a face-to-face would have required.

Moving the words from tape to paper is tricky. Slang words, pacing, emphasis, and cadence are all part of daily speech. Many of the people in this book are natural storytellers and they weave the language beautifully. They come from the north, south, midwest, and far west parts of the United States. One is from Chile. They are black, white, Hispanic. Some have big bucks and others are scrambling to make the rent from month to month.

Each person has a distinctive way of speaking, and I have tried to preserve that without having to resort to phonetic

16

spellings. Some accents, like South Carolinian and Deep Bronx, are impossible to bring to paper correctly. Also, most people do not speak in sharply defined sentences and paragraphs. Reporters come across this problem all the time, and you can see its effects in action by looking at two different newspapers' coverage of the same speech. In transposing my interviews, I've done my very best to stay true to the taped words and still make for good clear reading. I left in the ain'ts, the cuss words, the double negatives, and all the other warts. The beauty of English is not in some mummified classroom perfection, but in its ability to be slammed around in daily use and still come out shining and expressive. In the words of Canadian rockabilly genius Jack Scott, "The way I talk is just the way I talk."

■ DAN

It actually happened in the summer. It was warm and I was partying and stuff and I went home and there was somebody in my house. I lived in an apartment, second story. I got on in there and asked the guy, "What's going down, man, what are you doing in my shit?" What happened was he was like robbing my shit.

I said, "Hey man, no, no, no." I started pushing him around. He actually told me he was gonna shoot me and I didn't believe him. In them days it was like, if I beat you up, it's done, it's gone, I go home and patch my eye or whatever hurts the most, you know? At that time I was like eighteen, I was a young buck. You didn't just shoot people. There wasn't a drug thing at that time. Guys weren't shooting people over drugs. Drugs were just starting to happen big.

When I started pushing him around he says, "Man, leave me go or I'm gonna shoot you." I said, "Naw, you ain't gonna shoot me, man. I'll fuck you up, man." And the next thing you know he pulled a gun out.

What it was, I turned my back on him and started walking away. I said, "Fuck this, I'm throwing this motherfucker out." 'Cause I'd pushed him through two rooms, pushing him around. He was in my house robbing me. He pulled the gun out and just said, "Man, I'm gonna shoot you . . ." *Ba-boom*, man, he shot me in my face, hit me in my jaw, spun me around, and knocked me through a doorway.

I went through the door, the door wasn't closed, and I fell

on the ground. Now, he was three foot from me when he shot me, four foot maybe. When I hit the ground I felt my face, and I could feel the throbbing. It was throbbing, the shit was like pumping out of my face, out of the hole. I looked at my hands and it freaked me out. I said, "Wow, man, I'm fuckin' hurt."

You know if you're hurt, if you close your eyes maybe it's all a bad dream, maybe it'll go away when you open your eyes. I remember that part of it and I don't remember anything else.

There was a girl there, the girl that lived with me, and she come in and he was there standing over me with the gun and he's gonna shoot me again. He's like, "Yeah, I'm gonna blow your fuckin' head off."

Then she screamed. And he picked up the gun and pointed it at her and says, "I'm gonna shoot you, bitch." All of a sudden I come up off the floor, had him underneath in his crotch, had him by his throat, and just ran toward the window. Pushed him right through the window. He went out the second story window and down, fell on his back, broke his back. Today he's in a wheelchair.

Broke his back, know what I mean? The girl grabbed me by my pants and held me from falling out the window. I just laid there. She pulled me in. The police and ambulance came.

So I'm laying there, this is really good. This was a guy I know, a friend of mine, that's why I just pushed him around, smacked him around a little bit. You know, "What the fuck you doing?" So I'm in the hospital and the cops come and wanna talk to me about this, you know, and my mouth can't even move. My face looks like a basketball. They had these things down my throat so I could breathe, 'cause I couldn't breathe, my throat was swelled shut. So I'm laying there and my poor little sister come to see me, 'cause that's who they called, my sister. She's all crying and shit, man, and the cop's standing there telling, "Hey, the guy didn't shoot you in your arm, he didn't shoot you in your leg. He tried to blow off your fuckin' head. Do you understand that? He was trying to kill you. What are you gonna do about it?"

I said, "I can't wait to get outta this mess." That's the only thing I could say, 'cause I was naturally gonna take care of the situation.

But I could not be in the hospital. They didn't know if the guy had a couple bros or something. They went down and arrested him for shooting me, and they said, "We can't keep you in the area, which is this area here," so they took me to Walter Reed Army Hospital, 'cause I was in the service, you know.

That's where they opened my mouth and took pictures of the inside of my mouth, 'cause they couldn't believe that it didn't break through. See, it hit the jaw, ricocheted underneath my jaw, and lodged between my jugular vein and my vocal cords. They couldn't understand why it didn't shatter my jaw from that range, and why it didn't pierce the inside of my mouth.

All it did was, I lost a couple teeth and the thing was lodged in there. They wanted to operate on me. I didn't want to be in there because of the guys that were with me in the hospital room. Shit was shooting out of their throats. They'd hack, they had a hole in their throats so they could breathe, the hack shit would shoot out. It was like, "Wow, man," I was all fucked up from the drugs and all that. [One] guy had scars, 'cause, you know, he was in the service, this is military, he probably got hit by a bomb or something, one of them kind of guys. And that's what the whole ward was, nothing but head-up injuries. So I'm in there with all these kind of people, and the doc comes in and tells me that they were thinking about tomorrow I'll be able to get out of intensive care and they're gonna put me on a regular ward. I said, "Oh, well, that's cool." So my brother comes to see me and I get him to call these two girls I know. They come to see me and I have my clothes and stuff. . . . I was supposed to be in police custody because of the shooting. They'd shipped me all the way to Walter Reed to keep me from being in the area at the time.

These girls come down, they visit, take me down to the chapel, I change clothes, and we roll. And I'm back in the city here. I'm pretty freaked out about this thing that went down, I'm shot and all that shit. I talked to some friends and we're gonna roll on this dude. Know what I mean? Then I find out the guy's in a wheelchair. I mean to this day, he's still in a wheelchair. What are you gonna do to a guy that you've already paralyzed from the neck down?

He was a friend of mine. Nobody would break in your building but a friend, somebody who knew what you had and where you kept it. Why would somebody break in if he didn't know nothing? And why would he shoot me in the head, in the face? It was only a .25, but you take a .25 in your face and your mouth and you don't know where it's going.

I had it taken out about a year and a half later, 'cause when I walked out of the hospital the army kept calling my mom and telling her that I had to get back there because I was gonna get lead poisoning, I'm gonna die within a month or two. They called up and worried my mom to death. I worried my mom to death all her life, poor woman, but I mean this was the *army* calling my mom and telling her your boy gotta come back to the hospital, we gotta operate on him, we gotta get the lead out of him.

Today if I go to the dentist there's pieces of metal still in my jaw. Parts of it got over here where they had to cut it out, but the rest of it just fragged out. If you feel your bone there's not much underneath. See the dimple, see it there [left cheek]? That's where it went in. That's what fucked 'em up so much, that's why they wanted to take pictures of the inside of my mouth, 'cause they couldn't understand why it never pierced my mouth. It never pierced nothing. And it missed all the vital shit and lodged between the jugular vein and the vocal cords.

They couldn't figure this out. They were afraid to operate

on me because one way, if they would whoops, the jugular would be cut or the vocal cord. So they didn't want to operate right away, they wanted the swelling to go down so they'd know better what they were doing.

I went to the hospital and then it started scaring me because of the metal that was in there. The bullet shattered a tooth; half of it was still underneath and I didn't know it. About a year later all of a sudden my whole face swelled up. I thought I was missing the whole tooth and that was that. I was in a coma for a couple days, I was like under. I didn't know what was going on, and they had me in intensive care.

It's really funny, the whole situation. Look at you, then look at me. If they would have done what they did to you to my face . . . when you said your leg really looks good to you because you can use it, I pray to God about my face. Look at this; if I wouldn't have told you, you would never know.

When we got married and came here I didn't tell my wife [about] that. My friends started bringing it up: "Oh wow, did he tell you about the time he got shot in the face?" And she's like, "What? What are you talking about?" But she hung in there, she went with the punches. There's a lot of stuff I didn't tell her about my life. Then you'd run into somebody from your past and that story would come up, or this, how I got shot in the face and could have blown my fuckin' head off. Think if it would have been a .38 or .357.

That's what the man kept saying: "You're talking about a small caliber, you got lucky." Just the part where it didn't enter your mouth, how lucky can you be there?

When you're under the knife they do whatever they want. You have no control. When I was in that hospital in intensive care and I looked across and seen that guy, and seen the hoses that went in his nose to feed him, and the hole in his throat, and the scars on his face and stuff . . . that was one guy that, to this day, and I'm talking twenty years, still, I can see him. I was so freaked out from this guy that I couldn't stay in there. I had to look away, look out the window. I just couldn't handle it. I had to leave the hospital.

And I think that *by* leaving the hospital I saved myself a lot of aggravation and programming to make you better. As soon as I opened my eyes I could hear and see what was going on. They're in there with a camera taking pictures because all of a sudden I'm a guinea pig, I'm phenomenal. And you know the next step they would have had me under the knife, cutting me. After the swelling went down I got a break. If the swelling wouldn't have gone down they would have had to search 'cause the swelling would be all big. Naturally they would have to root around in there.

Well, I'm not into that. Not in my face. So I count myself lucky in that I was young and dumb and full of come, that I was hurt but I still got up and progressed. I was mad at the dude, I wanted to go get the dude. That was my main goal for leaving the hospital, even though I'm sure the secondary was like, hey, I don't even want to be in this room with these people.

In the hospital, when I first went in there, I blacked out. See, what happened was that I went into convulsions, this is what they told me, when the medical people came I was in convulsions, jerking around on the floor and shit after the girl pulled me in, from lack of blood. Every time my heart pumped it shot out. It wasn't clotting. I thought I was a goner.

When I got shot I thought I was dead. I found myself on the floor in another room. In fact I remember I turned around to go get this motherfucker and *psst*—I was on the floor and shit was pumping out of my face. When I looked up and my hands were both red and I seen like, he had me under the barrel, I was just, *"Fuck all this"* and passed out. Like a limbo sleep or something, to better my chance. Maybe I was thinking if I just lay here and not move maybe he'll think I'm like dead.

Then when I came up off the floor, at that time maybe 230, 240 pounds of trim beef, you know what I mean? I just picked him the fuck up and threw him right through the window. Not this way, but running with him, just *raaaaaa*, outraged, in a rage, berserk.

That's basically the story. It was this guy and he was in

there, he knew that I had some money and some herbs, and he was gonna clean me out 'cause I wasn't home. If you don't have no explanation and I see you with my gear in your pockets, shit that belongs to me, then I have no choice but to slap you the fuck around and find out what's going down. And he had no choice but to shoot me, 'cause I was hot. Like I said, I did throw him over a chair and a table, and flip him here and there a little bit. I'm not real good at somebody beating me, because I'm easy. I give. I'm a giver. But if you beat me I'm gonna beat you back. To this day I don't carry a gun, personally. My wife, she carries a gun, and she'll tell you what I tell her: "Hey, if you ever see anyone even want to touch me, you shoot him dead. You shoot him dead if he wants to touch me." I don't want no man to touch me ever again.

I ain't allowed to carry a weapon. I've been investigated by the alcohol and firearms people, all that bullshit, you know, in my lifetime, and I'm not allowed to have a weapon, be near a weapon, own a weapon, or anything like that because they think I'd shoot you.

That was the biggest traumatic thing in my life, being shot in the face. It gave me a big respect for people that reach for stuff, people that reach in their pocket, that turn on you quick. I'll drop you in a heartbeat. If I go sit somewhere, I always sit with my back toward something, a solid wall.

I never give a person a chance anymore. Before, I did. I was naive. Guy told me he was gonna shoot me, said, "I'm gonna blow your head off if you come near me again; you touch me again I'm gonna shoot you." I said, "Get the fuck outta here, I'm gonna kick your fuckin' ass." He pulled the gun out and shot me. So like whose fault is it? Should I have took heed, like back the fuck up and said, "Oh wow, man, don't shoot me?" Should I still have done what I done and get shot? I did know I was gonna be shot. It's not like the guy didn't tell me. What do you do? Hey, I'm gonna tear the motherfucker's head off. If I had to do it again I'd do it the same way. I'd get shot and still try to kill the guy.

24

If the guy wouldn't have broken his back and been para-lyzed, I'd be in jail for his death. Because I'd have found him, to the ends of the earth, and finished what I had to do.

When the man came in and rapped to me, when I woke up and all that, [they wanted me to] press charges against this guy. I didn't want to press charges against him. Because if he goes to jail I can't get him. I was young and dumb, man. I'm telling the man when I get out I'm gonna take care of it, in other words. That's stupid. 'Cause if the guy would have fell down and banged his head, they'd have come looking for me wondering why the guy fell down.

God teaches, God punishes, know what I mean? Look what happened to him and look what happened to me. Sometimes there is justice. In your case there's no justice; you got a scar to carry the rest of your life big time. I was a lucky kid. When I'm thinner, it shows up, so I would grow a beard.

I used to try and make jokes about it, like I was trying to catch a bullet in my mouth and misjudged and it hit me in the jaw. Why do you do it? Because you're ashamed to tell somebody, "Hey some junkie shot me."

No matter what happened, it's automatic: you did some-thing wrong also. Because it's never all one person's fault. You were involved in the drug scene, or whatever kind of scene it was—this is how people think. You tell them the story and this is what they try to read into it.

Dan lives in the eastern United States.

■ MICHAEL

Actually, this is pretty bizarre, because we were driving in a car out to a place to go shooting and I told my friends something was going to happen to me. It involved my left thigh. I didn't know what it was, or anything. So I handed my friend the keys when I got out of the car because I knew something was going to happen to me.

We were out collecting mistletoe, and I was climbing trees and that, and we were shooting. This was southern California, out by Ramona. We'd headed out on a dirt road for a good hour. Charlie hands me the gun and says, "Shoot it." We were shooting at targets. The gun popped and stayed open. I looked into it and I didn't see anything. I handed it back to him and said, "It's unloaded." He looked at me and said, "It's empty?" I said, "Yeah, I think it's empty," and I pulled out a knife and laughed and said, "Knives never run out of ammunition."

He laughed and waved the gun at me, pulled the trigger, and it went off.

I was on acid. And it was real interesting, because I closed my eyes . . . you get shot with a .22 even a foot and a half, two feet away, and it'll spin you around. I closed my eyes when I was spinning around, and all I could see was Marshal Dillon hitting me with like a .45 and taking my leg off . . . hitting me dead center in the femur. Didn't see a thing, just closed my eyes and all I could see was my leg was blown off.

Once I stopped being turned around I pulled my pants

open and looked at it and the entrance hole was all black and the exit hole had a lot of meat hanging out and it was smokin'. The first thing I did was look up and say, "Well, there's something you don't see in the movies. It's still smokin'."

I decided I'd better run, get out of there. I put my fingers in the entrance and exit holes and ran up the hill about a quarter of a mile on one leg, one knee, and two elbows. I got to the top of the hill, pulled my fingers out, realized I wasn't bleeding, looked back down and said, "Okay, I'm all right. Let's get me out of here."

Meanwhile, the guy who shot me panicked and threw the gun away. I told him, "We're not leaving here without the gun. Go back and get the goddamn gun. I'm okay. We've just gotta drive out of here." So he went back down and got the gun. We drove for a while until we found some guys on a telephone pole and said where's the nearest clinic and they told us Ramona.

This is like a twenty-minute ride on a bumpy road, which hurts like hell the whole time. I decided that since he'd shot me, Charlie was going to get it from me for the whole entire trip. So I bitched at him the entire trip, saying, "You asshole, what the fuck did you do that for?" He finally got tired of listening to me and I said, "That's cool, I'm tired of talking."

The first place we found was this Indian clinic, and the Indians did *not* want to deal with me. The doctor said, "Well, we'll put you in another room and we'll X-ray you and see if there's anything in there." There wasn't. So they left me alone with the tools and said, "You've gotta clean it out yourself." So I did. I stuck the probe completely through and pulled it back out. It didn't collect anything, so I decided that's that. I never got a stitch. When I got back to the city I went to a doctor and he said there was nothing he could do.

I heard my friend calling my father and my father asking him where I was shot, and Jeff says, "Out by Ramona." And my father says, "No, *where* was he shot?" And Jeff says, "By the cable crossing." I'm saying, "Jeff, you asshole, tell him where I was shot on my body." Jeff says, "Oh, where on his body. Through his thigh, through the meaty part of his thigh. He didn't hit anything and there's no bleeding. He's okay."

When we were leaving to go back out to the car the sheriff finally showed up and asked, "Is there any bad blood between you two guys?" We said no. He said, "Is there any reason this guy would have shot you?" I said, "No not at all, actually. It was just an accident. Empty gun, ha ha."

I've read a couple magazines from the Civil War, and what they said during the Civil War was that a bullet wound will kill you. If it don't kill you straight out it'll kill you for the rest of your life. Which is true, because every time it rains I can feel it. The weather changed last night. I could feel it. I was leaving school, UCLA, going, "Oh my God," 'cause I can feel it straight through.

The best part . . . when he shot me, he waved the gun and pulled the trigger, and it hit me in the [fly] button, which was right by the crotch, pushed everything back, and went in. Without the button it would have hit the femoral artery, which is right there. It ricocheted off the button. . . . It was still moving fast enough that it cauterized the wound completely and there was no blood.

I was stabbed in 1968 by Black Panthers, in the throat. There were five of them that were really worth screwing with. One of them, the first guy, was standing in front of me, doodling on my chest with his knife, through my shirt, making nice little scars. I looked down, I was leaning against a telephone pole, and thought: "I'm gonna die, but I'm gonna take somebody with me." I stomped on his foot and brought my knee up between his legs and he fell over. I turned to the second guy and brought my foot straight up between his legs and heard something crack like eggs and watched him turn white and fall over. The third guy lashed straight out with the knife. It went straight in and clipped a salivary gland, so I had to have a doctor go in and clean up the wound and pull out the salivary gland. It was a bitch, especially at a navy hospital.

When I was twelve I had cornea surgery at a naval hospital. The guy in the bed across from me had been hit by machine gun fire. He had over fifty holes in him. He was screaming most of the time we were there. They had him doped up on morphine completely, but he was still screaming the whole time. Sometime around ten o'clock at night his screaming turned to moaning, then about twelve o'clock the moaning turned to a gurgling rattle, and after one o'clock there wasn't any more noise. Six in the morning they drug him out. That's really great when you're twelve years old, it's a really impressive thing to watch somebody croak right in front of you.

Michael enjoys life in Southern California.

▪ FRANK

Start with the situation, the way things were. Let's go back to the '60s. In the '60s, what was happening, there were the original families. One family, one of the original families, ran most of Brooklyn. It was run by a man named Joe Profaci. He was an original boss after the Luciano breakup. Profaci, at that time, had no street-smart capos. He had Joe Columbo, who you know all about, and a few guys, but none of them were really street-smart tough guys. They were called "Fat Cat Americans." They weren't used to a toe-to-toe war.

It's always been the habit of bosses to have one family, one group, that were shooters, that were guys that just liked to do this shit. In fact there's a family in Sicily that does nothing but that, I forget the name, but they're paid by contributions from the five families. They have no active involvement except they're gunsels. If you read the papers now, Gotti used these Westies that come from around here [Hell's Kitchen, New York City] for the same purpose. Which is a mistake; you don't use Irishmen.

Anyway, Joe Profaci, he had a lot of trouble with the black element as far as numbers. You couldn't run a numbers operation without blacks as runners, local collectors, that kind of shit, but they answer to the Italians. He was having a lot of trouble keeping them in line. Joe Columbo would say, "Hey, you're skimming." And that'd be the end of it. He needed somebody to say, "Hey, you're skimming . . . *pow.*"

So he hooks up with a group of brothers called the Gallo

brothers. The movie *The Gang That Couldn't Shoot Straight* was a parody about them. They came from President Street. The Gallo brothers: Crazy Joe, Al the Blast, and the smart one, I always forget his name, and I know him as well as I know my own brother . . . Larry Gallo. They had a crew and they used to answer directly to Profaci. You gotta understand, they weren't made. They were not made members in the sense that they could not rise in rank, they were not members of the family.

He used the Gallo brothers. The strength of the Gallo brothers was in South Brooklyn, where they came from, that area of President Street, they were invincible. I don't care if you were Gambino or whoever you were; in that neighborhood, they were law. They had, like the old days, they had the people. When you have that sense of neighborhood backing, it's invaluable for a crew like this.

Maybe I'm dragging this out, but it's all to show you how war starts. At the same time, in the other families, there's a political problem brewing with a guy named Vito Genovese. He's coming out of prison and he wants to take over his family. The problem was his family was being run by a guy named Frank Costello. Frank Costello was called the Prime Minister, and he was a thinking boss, he wasn't a shooter. Frank Costello had an ace in his pocket, and he was a guy named Albert Anastasia.

Albert Anastasia was a Mad Hatter. I used to wash his car in Brooklyn. He was a total homicidal maniac, a man without conscience, rhyme, or reason. But he had a devotion to Costello that went back to when they were childhood friends. Costello used to help him when they were kids. The character in *The Godfather* of Luca Brasi, that character, that devotion, was based on Anastasia's devotion to Costello.

So Vito Genovese sends word from prison, he says, "I'm coming back, I'm taking over the family. Costello, you're out." Costello says, "Well, I'll work with you, what the hell." "No, you're out, I don't want you. Just step away."

Costello says, "Well, hey, wait a minute." One word leads

to another, and Anastasia says, "I don't give a fuck who Vito Genovese is, how tough he is. He gets out of prison and I'm gonna kill him." P.S. he goes and gets a shave and a haircut. . . . It was a shoot done by the Gallo brothers. The Gallo brothers whacked out Albert Anastasia.

At the time I was fifteen, sixteen years old. I worked for Joe Gallo, and I headed his numbers in that area of South Brooklyn and Bensonhurst, he had a small enclave of Bensonhurst. I used to just collect for him. I didn't have any kind of authority, but I collected for him. The Gallo brothers do this hit now, they whack out Anastasia, Vito Genovese is almost killed by Carmine Gigante, you know this guy The Chin? Almost killed by him, but for whatever reason he misses. Genovese comes out and the family becomes the Genovese family. At that time, before Genovese, it was known as the Luciano family.

Now the Gallo brothers go back to Profaci. The thing went from Genovese in jail to Profaci. Profaci turned it over to the Gallo brothers. They whack out Anastasia and leave a clean path for Genovese to take over his family. The Gallo brothers go back to Joe Profaci and say, "All right, now we want what you promised us." He promised them better territory, and he promised them they'd be made. The three Gallo brothers would be made.

They were a little worried about Joe Gallo. See, the thinker was Larry Gallo. Al Gallo, Al the Blast—the Blast was like a nickname that he took—he really was nothing. Larry was a thinker, he was a smart man. Joey Gallo, they didn't call him Crazy Joe because he was sane. He was psychotic. They were very worried about him.

Anyway, they go back and tell Profaci, "Give us what you promised us." Joe Profaci and this other guy named Maggliocco, they reneged on their promise. And instead this guy Joe Columbo—the whole reason they hired the Gallo brothers was that Columbo was such a fucking mutt—they make him a capo. Not only do they make this guy a capo, Joe Columbo, they put him over the Gallo brothers. You have to understand, this is that Italian mentality, like a discipline: "We're not ready to do what we told you we'd do. You do as we say. Don't do as we do, do as we say."

They reneged on this thing. Joe Gallo says, "Okay, fine." Joe Columbo comes to them and says, "I don't want no trouble with you Gallos. They made me the boss, I'm the boss. But meanwhile I'm gonna back you guys up, I'm gonna fight for you guys. I'll get you what you want. Just let me know what you're gonna do."

Joe Gallo says, "You know what we're gonna do? We're gonna go to war with Profaci. We're gonna kidnap him."

They couldn't kidnap him because Joe Columbo goes back to Profaci and tells him what's gonna happen. So they kidnap his nephew, Joe Profaci's nephew.

Next thing you know: war. Big shooting war. Goes on for like two, three weeks. Joe Columbo's a stool pigeon. They shoot, kill a couple of Columbo's cronies, they kill a couple of Profaci's cronies. The reason I got into this was my cousin. My father's brother's daughter married a guy named Lolly. In fact, if you remember, if you ever read *The Gang That Couldn't Shoot Straight*, they had Big Jelly. [He] actually existed. This guy was my cousin, I call him a paper cousin, Lolly. But again, he was psychotic. You have to understand, most of these guys that get in a shooting war and do that kind of stuff, you gotta have one screw loose. He was in the Korean War. The earliest memory I have of Lolly is that he shows me a picture of him in Korea, he was a paratrooper. He's got his gear on, and he's got Kotex pads under the gear; they used to put them under the gear so when they dropped on the old parachutes, they'd absorb. They made the best cushions. *He's got fuckin' heads under his arms!* Two North Korean heads under his fuckin' arms. I mean, that's. . . .

Anyway, the war starts. Big, big shooting war. They asked for loyalty. I said, "Lolly, what the fuck are we doing over here? I don't care how crazy or tough the Gallos are." Lolly gives me a smack, says, "You're with the Gallos, you're gonna die with the Gallos." Now, I may have been tough but

I wasn't psychotic. I wasn't ready to give my life for my country, let alone three brothers from President Street.

But it's too late. Profaci's already laid down the law and they drew a line. I was on the end of that line. So now the government steps in, the city police step in, and they put the Gallos under civil arrest. This means they're arrested in their houses and they're under police protection. They simply did this to stop the war, because bodies were falling all over the street. Not only that, this was a time when the families had a controlling interest in the police department. It doesn't exist that much now, but in those days, the Profacis were losing, so they went to the cops and said, "Lock these guys up." So they put a civil arrest.

There was two famous houses on President Street, President and Carrolton, I forget the cross street, but it was right on President Street, that's where the Gallos were holed up. The shooting with me was, we were painting; we were supposedly painting the insides of the place so the cops would let you in and out. I mean there was cops, detectives, uniform cops, the whole block was sealed off. I mean, we were like heroes, folk heroes. Not me in particular, but the quote "Gallo Gang." So now we had to get guns up there because at night, we'd sneak out. So they needed guns. The cops would come in, shake you down every other day. So Joey sets up something in Vermont, he's got guns coming in from Vermont. Pistols. So now we gotta get 'em into the thing. We're gonna paint the place, and we're gonna paint the place because of the paint cans. We have the guns wrapped in plastic, and each paint can has a gun. No problem. But we have more paint cans than paint.

So that's what we do, we get everybody armed. The war is still going on, but it's going on under the watchful eye of the police. They send me out one night to make a collection. You can't operate a war without money. So they send me out to make a collection from some niggers. If you remember anything about the Gallos, he had blacks in his crew. That was the kiss of death for the wops. But Crazy Joe was Crazy

Joe, he didn't give a fuck about anything.

I was only sixteen years old, maybe seventeen then, but I'd just gotten out of high school. It started when I was in St. John's Prep. I was out of high school when it finished up. So they sent me out, I'm leaving, and in the course of events I get contacted by a guy named Persico. There's two Persicos. One just died. Allie Boy just died of cancer about a year or two ago. And Carmine the Snake. Carmine the Snake contacts me. You gotta understand that at seventeen you're very impressionable. I wanted to be a shooter. I wanted to wear fedoras as soon as they didn't look silly on me, silk suits, that kind of stuff. So Carmine contacts me and says, "We got a situation for you. Mr. Profaci thinks you're an okay kid. He wants you to come in with us. But we need somebody inside to know what these scumbags are doing. What do you think of that?"

I said, "I don't know, I gotta think about this." At seventeen, it's a fuckin' decision to make. These guys are my friends. Do I step on 'em, don't I step on 'em, whatever.

He says, "All right, what we want you to do," he says, "we want you to find out who will come with you. Who inside is sick of Joe Gallo and who will come with you." So they set up a meet. "Bring whoever will come with you."

At seventeen I wasn't about to talk to anybody. All it was was a setup. Whoever would come with me, that was three they could whack out, two they could whack out. They had no plans at all to make peace.

I went by myself. I didn't talk to Lolly, I didn't talk to Joe Gallo, I didn't talk to anybody. I didn't even know what the fuck I was doing. I just went back to this meeting. I talked to one guy named Andy Boy, he was my age. Andy Boy was his nickname; his name was Michael. Mike Romeo. But anyway, I went, and I told Mike Romeo I was going. He said, "Holy shit, what're you gonna do?" I said, "I don't know, I'm just gonna run away for a few months. Fuck it, I don't want to get in the middle of this."

It was a no-win situation, and I wasn't smart enough. So I

decide to go meet Carmine Persico. I go where I'm sup-posed to go, and I'll never forget at the time I had a '65 white Pontiac.

And I show up. Two cars pull up and they want to know who's with me, and nobody's with me, and all of a sudden next thing I know somebody says, "*I'll kill that little cock-sucker.*" And there's fuckin' guns coming out and I'm run-ning, and I have no gun on me and I'm running. You gotta understand, nobody's a marksman with this stuff. In general these guys are not marksmen. When you hit somebody you walk right up to 'em and blow 'em away. So you really don't have too much target practice. I mean, you see how many guys they sent to shoot Castellano.

So there's guns firing and I'm running, scared shit. I must have left a trail of liquid dung behind me. Scared shit. And I get shot in the leg.

Funny thing about getting shot in the leg—and you know better than me because you wound up with much more damage than I did. When you got shot it was immediately obvious that you were hurt, I would guess. You got back to the building and so on, but you knew something serious was going on. The thing with me was I knew something serious could happen if I didn't keep moving. I got shot over here [outside of leg]. I got an entry wound. The bullet came out, the exit wound is no longer visible. I would imagine it was a small-caliber bullet.

My immediate thought was, *This ain't shit.* You know when your adrenaline is pumping from fear, maybe you think clearer than you normally would, or maybe you think dumber than you normally would, but I thought, *I can handle this shit.* Like I'm a boxer getting in the ring with Mike Tyson and catching two shots from him, still standing and saying, "What's this guy?" My biggest fear in that profession was be-ing killed. You get killed because you get shot, basically. Get-ting shot in the leg, I remember running and saying, "Oh, that's nothing." Not realizing that a fucking leg wound . . . a shot in the back of the head is a whole different story.

That was my immediate thing. Later on, the fear of being shot never sunk in as much as the fear of being killed. Now this is kind of a contradiction in terms, but the fact that I got away from being killed, it never dawned on me that I was shot and I survived. It dawned on me that I was in this fucking situation and I got shot. It never bothered me, the bullet. If anything, the nightmares from then—and they're not nightmares—that stay in the back of my head, was the amount of fuckin' lead that was flyin' around that street . . . it's a cobblestone street, the beginning or the ass end, depending on how you're coming, of South Brooklyn. Carrol Street, President Street. Their area was right next to the Brooklyn-Queens Expressway, this is closer to the water. You got the BQE, this stretch of these streets, then you have the water with Bush Terminal, where the old navy yard used to be. So it's right in between there, where it happened.

I went to the hospital with the wound; there was fuckin' blood all over the place. This was a pussy wound compared to what you got, you have to understand. But still a lot of blood. Did you put your hand on it when you got shot? What was your feeling of the flesh? I remember my hand being cold, ice cold.

I had no fear about the wound. My biggest fear was the set of circumstances that got me there. How the fuck do I explain this now? After thinking about it for a while I was very happy I didn't tell anybody or bring anybody because then I could make up any story I wanted. Then I figured, well, I'll tell 'em the truth—they told me to bring everybody and I went by myself. Then I thought about Joey Gallo and said, holy shit, no matter what I tell this fuckin' maniac he's not gonna believe me. Why did I talk to him, why didn't I tell him, why why why? Then I said I won't tell anybody, but what do I say about this fuckin' bullet wound. Then I say, well, fuck it, let me see what I can do.

So now I go to the emergency room. I leave my car where it is. By the time I ran I was closer to, say, going to the Verrazano Bridge. It's nighttime, but you've got a gigantic black stain on black jeans. And you can feel that warmth, that stickiness. I was walking on the leg, so I knew there wasn't that kind of problem. I called Andy, Mike Romeo, and I had him pick me up.

Now, you've gotta understand, you're talking about two survives. You want to survive the bullet wound, which I really didn't think was that bad, because I managed to run. I'm also figuring they're scouring the neighborhood for me, which is bullshit because once they miss a hit they go and do what they got to do. It's not like the police department putting out an APB—they want to get out of there. Now I called Andy, and I remember before I called him, preparing my story. You want to be consistent with these people. I call Andy and I say, "These cocksuckers tried to kill me. I want a gun, bring me down a gun. I'll blow their fucking heads off." So he comes down and takes me to Coney Island Hospital. I walk in and the guy asks what happened, and I say, "I don't know, I fell down and my leg's all bleeding, I was in a lot . . ." When you're seventeen or sixteen you don't lie very good, falling down and getting a fucking wound right through your leg.

I'll never forget, and it pissed the shit out of me, I mean, the pants have a hole in 'em, they're loaded with blood, but the guy goes right away and cuts the pants. And I'm thinking, *why didn't he just let me take my pants off?* So stupid.

Cuts the pants, he's looking at it, uses the probe and he's fucking around the exit wound, pressing on it, probing it . . . it wasn't really a bad wound. He was telling me I was lucky, it missed this, that, and the other, and then he looks me straight in the face—and he was not an Indian, but he looked like an Indian, a Pakistani, whatever—but he looks me straight in the face and says, "Oh, it's a bullet wound." I said, "What the fuck are you talking about?" (laughs)

The funny thing about a bullet wound, at least, this particular bullet wound, you can't stitch them. I don't know what they do now, but then they put like a butterfly, they put it in and it clamps the skin together like tape. Antiseptic, all that red shit all over the wound, this, that, and the other, and then of course they gotta make out a police report.

The police have gotta be called in, so they send you back to the waiting room to sit down, and the cop comes over, sat down, and said, "I'd like to make a report on that."

"On what? I fell in a lot."

"But the doctor in the emergency room says it's a bullet wound."

I said, "Nah, nah, but could you call my mother and father and get 'em here?" I gave the cop the phone number. He says, "All right, you stay here."

I'll never forget this cop, and it shows you what a prick you can be under certain circumstances. He says, "Listen to me. I'm supposed to take you into a room and handcuff you, according to procedure." I said, "Where am I gonna go? Look at me." He says, "All right, stay here, I'll call your mother and father . . . but I want you to be honest with me." I said, "All right, all right."

The minute that fucking cop left I said, "*Andy, let's get the fuck outta here!*" And we ran away.

End of story. I never went back, the thing healed itself, and I have an entry wound here that I can still see.

Frank lives well and prospers in New York City.

■ TRAVIS BECK

I was at a place called CCN, South Vietnam. I was leading teams of Green Berets and Vietnamese mercenaries on reconnaissance missions along the Ho Chi Minh Trail in Laos. We would go to a launch site, at Quang Tri, and if the weather was right we'd go into Laos. I was there with my team, and the weather was right, and the helicopters would come there to pick us up. We'd already had our final briefing, and I went back down to our main tent to get everything together and lay down on the cot and take a five minute nap. Like a boxer before a fight or something.

My little people were cooking as they always did. Anytime they had a second to spare they would squat down and pinch off some C-4 and heat up some of their indigenous rations. One of the rations they had was tiny little minnows, dried minnows, that they cook up and mix with rice. It really smelled terrible.

As soon as I laid down I woke up with a tremendous cramp in my leg. I tried to stand up and fell. I could smell what I thought was those fish cooking. I grabbed the back of my thigh and I looked at my hand and it was bloody. I thought at first I'd been shot with a silenced weapon.

Amazingly, one of my little people, Vietnamese, picked me up and carried me a couple hundred yards to the tactical operations base. I'm a big person, and I didn't think that they were capable of doing that. But this one did. He ran up there with me and they brought a stretcher out.

I laid down on the stretcher and that's a sensation that's unexpected, when you're lying on a stretcher on the ground and you're at boot-top level looking up. And I was looking up at an incredible assortment of faces, all these Vietnamese and Montagnard mercenaries, all sorts of interesting people looking down. My team was around me, and my team leader was kneeling beside me, his knees were against my thigh, and he was rocking back on his heels, putting the top of his head on my chest, rocking back and forth and crying and saying that he'd shot me.

It was really bizarre. They were pretty emotional people anyway, and I had a lot of friends among the Montagnards and they were very upset. A really strange, strange scene.

They loaded me up on a truck and we went to the field hospital at Quang Tri, which was a hospital designed to handle massive casualties. It was one of the main points that casualties would be evacuated back to in case of a big battle. I was virtually the only one in there when I went in. It was really depressing, like a slaughterhouse. All the floors were sloped to these huge drains, and all the instruments could slide back and forth along steel rods, up and down. It could handle thousands of people, I'm sure.

They whacked my clothes off and wheeled me into the place and I waited for a while. They X-rayed me, then this doctor came out and showed me a picture of a pen flare and asked me if I knew what it was; it was in my leg. I told him what it was and he was wondering if it was going to explode.

A pen flare, I should say, is a flare that recon teams use. The entire flare is like a .45 automatic round, jacket and shell casing, the entire .45 automatic round. It has a screw attachment on the bottom and you screw it down on what looks like a nail set. The cone of the nail set is spring loaded. You just screw it down on there and flip the spring-loaded thing and it would ignite the flare. It burns magnesium and takes off and looks just like a tracer round. Identical to a tracer round. That's what my interpreter had shot me with, a pen flare, and it burned out in my leg.

They operated on me from behind sandbags in case it blew up. They didn't know if it was completely burned out or not. But I'm sure that they got so much exotic shit in there inside people that they just had their standard operating procedure for any unexploded ordnance that was inside people. And that was it.

I was in the hospital for a year. It cut a nerve in my leg, and because of all the magnesium particles they left it open from my knee to my ass for three months trying to get all the infection to clear up.

[From the shooting, Travis got drop foot.] There is a chance of that coming back for about a year. After that, if it doesn't, the muscles will be gone to the point that even if the nerves come back it won't do you any good. That's why I was in the hospital so long; they did another operation to go in there and see what had happened to the nerve before the time ran out. There was nothing they could line up in there. I've always wondered maybe if the circumstances of their operating were what gave me drop foot.

But actually, drop foot, historically, since ancient times, it's always been a penetrating wound that gives people drop foot. It used to be real common when people were riding horses and getting shot with arrows. Arrows penetrating the leg gave people drop foot. Spears and arrows made it a real common disease. Nowadays a bullet wound is virtually the only way you can get it.

Travis Beck lives in his native north Texas.

■ RANDY WALKER

I thought for a long time I wasn't going to make it. They lost me twice. This is what happened. My brother was running around with my friend's wife. But I didn't know that. And I didn't know really at the time what was going on. I caught my friend's wife over at my brother's house one night. I was over there and she come up. I told her to get the hell on down the road, don't be coming out here no more or she'd be causing trouble.

Therefore, she cussed me something or other and she left. Next thing I know she and my brother started seeing each other hot and heavy. But I didn't know that was going on. I didn't see it nor hear nothing about it. I just told her that one time I caught her at it, "Don't come around here, you going to cause trouble."

So the next thing I know her husband was going to shoot my brother. Went up to his office and pulled a gun on him and all this stuff, said he'd blow his ass away right there in the office. Needless to say the boy didn't do it. So they called my brother up there a couple nights later and told him they was gonna burn all our houses down and all our businesses down. That they was gonna stop the Walkers. They had the money to do it. My brother come over to my house and told me about it and I said, "Don't worry about it. Just go on home." I said, "I'll call Larry"—that was the girl's husband, the friend of mine. I said, "I'll call Larry and I'll talk to Larry and I'll get all this thing straightened out.

This is no big deal." I said, "You shouldn't have been messing with his wife."

Therefore I called Larry to talk to him. And I couldn't get him on the phone, so I said, "I'll ride down there and see him. Ain't no big deal." So I drove down there to his house, and drove up to his house and got out. I knocked on the door and nobody answered. I stood there for a few seconds, you know, just like normal. Knocked on the door again and nobody answered. So I said, "Hell, there's nobody home." I walked back and got in my car and went to drive off. So I got going out of the place and when I did this truck blocked me in. Coming down the road there's two oak trees on the side and the truck slid across the front of my car coming out. Next thing I know these two fellas jumped out and just started shooting.

They shot my car about eight or nine times there, with shotguns and a pistol. It was Larry and his daddy, the boy's daddy. So they leaned into the car and they pulled me out. The stuck a .357 Magnum . . . well, before they pulled me out they had a shotgun, they got to the car after shooting the car so many times, walking up to me the whole time. I was down on the floorboard of the car. They got to the car and one of 'em stuck a shotgun in the car window on one side and one stuck a .357 Magnum in the other side, up in my head. Larry had a shotgun on me and his daddy walked around the other side of the car, and when he got around the other side of the car, on the driver's side, he pulled me out. He stuck that .357 inside, punched it right in my skin [left side of belly], and pulled the trigger.

When he pulled the trigger I didn't fall. I was still leaning up against the car then. And Larry went running around like he was crazy, "*Oh my God, Daddy, you killed Randy.*" They thought it was my brother, but it wasn't my brother; it was me. It was nighttime, it was dark, they couldn't see. It all happened so fast, when they blocked my car in they just started shooting. And they pulled me out and they shot me. So Larry went running around there crazy as hell, "Oh my

God, Daddy, you killed Randy, you shot Randy."

So Larry, he left. I didn't know where he went. And the old man, says, "I'm gonna take and"—this is what he's saying out loud—says, "I'm gonna take and put him in the car and put the car outside on the road there, like somebody just pulled up there and shot him and drove off." So when he went to do that I said, "Oh hell no you not. You shot me here and I'm gonna stay here." So I fought the old man, and I fought him till all the blood pumped out my body. And when it finally pumped out my body I hit the ground.

And I was lying there on the ground there, and Mr. Blocker was walking around me saying, "Well, I got one. Now if I can get his brother and his daddy, that'll eliminate all the problems for the Blockers. That'll do away with the Walkers." He was walking around me kicking me and stuff while I was laying there on the ground. So I stayed there about two hours, I reckon, all the blood pumped out of me. I was drowning in my own blood when the [ambulance] came.

The ambulance was taking me on to the hospital over there in Charleston, at the university. And right before they got me there, they lost me. Then they brought me back around the time they pulled in; they put some kind of bag or something on. They brung me back around. So while they was operating on me they lost me again. They told my parents that I was dead, that I died, that they couldn't do nothing about it, couldn't save me. Two and a half hours later they went back and told them that they brung me back around.

So I laid up for about fourteen months. I lost 49 percent of my insides: my pancreas, my spleen, some of my intestinals, some of my colon, two-thirds of my stomach, my kidney, and a few things I can't even say 'em. That's all gone, all out of there. Just about everything on my left side. The only thing left on my left side is my lung. I got both lungs. I only got one kidney. No spleen, none of that, no pancreas.

Either the spleen or the pancreas keeps your body from getting infected. Like if you got a cold it wouldn't hurt you, but if I got a cold I could get pneumonia and die, 'cause I have nothing to fight off infection. If you got a cut on your arm it'll probably heal up right away. If I get a cut on my arm it'll probably take forever for it to heal up. I have nothing in my system to fight off infection. You do, I don't.

I had two plastic bags and four tubes sticking out my body for months and months. When I was laid up I caught hell. I still catch hell. I'm tired all the time. I'm tired before I get out the bed, I'm tired when I get in. If I don't do nothing all day I'm still tired. If I work hard as I can go I'm still tired. I'm just tired twenty-four hours a day.

This was April the second, 1987. Three years this April went by. I can still move as much, but I get tired. I used to never get tired. Tired wasn't in my vocabulary; I didn't know what the word meant. I could go from daylight to dark and still I wasn't tired. Now I'm just tired all the time. It's like I'm pulling a trailer. I have to take vitamins and stuff all the time for this and that.

He stuck that gun in me and pulled the trigger. Stuck it in me right in the skin and pulled the trigger. That's like throwing a grenade in a box, that's how it did my insides. I never hit the ground until all the blood pumped out my body. When they got to me they said something like 5 percent of the blood was left in my body.

How'd they find me? Well, come to find out Larry, when he left there, when his daddy shot me and he was running around crazy, saying "Oh my God, Daddy, you killed Randy," he went and called EMS. He had enough sense to call. See it wasn't meant for me. Me and him was friends. They had no idea they shot me. They thought they shot my brother in my car, and I reckon they thought, in their eyes, that that was my brother coming up there to see Larry's wife and he just used my car to throw off the, you know how it is. I just went down there to talk. I didn't have a knife, I didn't have a stick, I didn't have a gun, I didn't have nobody with me. Absolutely nothing in the car but me. That's why it looked so bad on them, because they tried to say to the law that, you know, Randy was coming down there to cause trouble because he would kick ass and take names later.

They figured it was my brother, but they made sure that nobody was gonna kick ass. If anybody kicked ass it was gonna be them. Me and my brother's like day and night. He wears suits all the time. He just has somebody to do it, to do what he wants. He don't dirty his hands. He don't even cut his own grass, somebody else cuts his grass. Whatever needs to be done, he gets somebody else to do it. He don't do nothing. He's an accountant and a real estate agent.

They tried to tell the law that I come up there to burn their places and stuff down. They tried to reverse the role of what they told my brother. See, they told my brother a couple days before, they walked into his office and told him they was gonna burn our houses and our businesses down. After they shot me and found out it was me, they reversed it and said, "Paul called"—that's my brother—"Paul called and said Randy's coming up there to burn y'all's houses down, and y'all's businesses." But see it wasn't like that because I didn't have nothing in the car.

I told them, I said, "I had a convict, an ex-convict right there at my house the same night I went over there. If I wanted to cause trouble I would have took him because he's good at it. But I sent him home." He even testified, he said, "I told Randy I would go with him but Randy said no, he'd go by hisself because there would be trouble. If he went by hisself there wouldn't be trouble." That's why I went by myself. Didn't have a gun, knife, stick, nothing. That right there shows you I didn't go there to cause no trouble. Because if I went there to cause trouble you can bet I would have caused it. I've been known to do it.

They said I'd never work again, and hell, I work every day. They said I wouldn't do this, and I do that thing. I'm just twice as tired. I'm just tired as hell. They just put me in a little slower gear. I still do basically everything.

They had machines, about seventeen machines stuck in my body keeping me living. A lot of stuff I just blocked out.

My family, nobody brings it up around my family on the outside. But my family gets together and they talk, but they don't talk around me. Because I don't want to hear it. I told them, "It's over with. What's done is done. Y'all want to talk, y'all want to discuss what went on between y'all," like a lot of stuff I don't even know about because they wouldn't tell me. When I come around three months later and I couldn't remember what they was talking about, I'd tell 'em I didn't want to hear it. They'd walk out of the hospital room or go somewhere and talk about it, but they never talk around me because I didn't want to hear it. My mother knows three times as much as I know. I don't know nothing because I just blocked it out. I didn't want to hear it. I was too busy worrying about living to worry about what the hell happened and what went down.

For like a year, I really didn't remember what happened. I was just concentrating on one thing and that was getting better. Anything else didn't exist. I didn't care who you was, how tall you was, how wide you was, what you looked like, where you come from. I didn't worry about none of that stuff. I didn't worry about paying my bills. All I worried about was helping Randy. That's what I dedicated my time to for a year and something.

I remember dying, though. I remember dying. I don't remember dying when I was in the hospital and they was operating on me, but right before they got me to the hospital I was like in a lot of pain, and I was miserable. I didn't know a human body could take so much and still survive. But right before I died, it's like I wasn't hurting. I wasn't scared of nothing. Everything was just as smooth as it could be. Next thing I knew, it was gone. I was at peace when I died.

I never had that peace of mind in my life, as easy as I was. I wasn't scared no more. Like before, when they first picked me up, I was scared. I was scared to *death*. I was in a state of shock. But right before I died I was just as calm . . . nothing worried me, everything was all right. Never, ever have I experienced anything like that. And I hope to God it's a long time before I have to experience it again.

What it really is, I faced reality. I knew I was going. You knew you had to do what you had to do. It's like you didn't have no choice. It wasn't that you give up, I never give up, but I knew it wasn't in my hands to say whether I make it or don't make it. I was beyond that point. That is, if I die and they bring me back around, if I make it, I make it. There wasn't no fright or nothing. Oh my God I'm gonna die? Before when I was in all that pain and stuff, that was running across my mind, "I'm gonna die, I know I'm gonna die," I was telling myself, "I'm gonna die." And I did. But right before I died I stopped worrying about it. If I die, I die, if I don't, I don't. And everything's all right with me, I'm all right with everybody. I was just as chilled out as I could be.

You appreciate [life] now, but before you didn't. It seemed like before everything was pure hell, but you liked it like that. But now everything's a lot easier, a lot sweeter. You're glad you got it. Before it didn't matter if you had it or not, the hell with it.

Now, if I have a feud with somebody, I walk off and forget about it. Unless it's a big one, then I send somebody else. You ain't gotta worry about me coming around, but somebody'll contact you. Somebody'll rattle your cage a little bit. I try to do everything now I possibly can to help people. I see life a lot different. Like before I was a little hellion, the hell with this and the hell with that. I really didn't have no respect for nothing myself. But now I do. Like I'll see kids do things sometimes and I'll say, "Son, you ought not do that." Uptown or something, he's doing something he's got no business doing. He's cussing me, he says, "Mind your own damn business. Don't tell me what to do; you ain't my parents." Stuff like that, and I'm thinking, I was the same years ago. If only he knew what he was doing to himself.

That's like, before, I'd drink. Now I don't drink. I don't go to bars, I don't go where no drinking is. I go to work and

I come home, go to work, come home. That's every day of my life. I don't go out to eat, I don't ever go out to eat. Me and my fiancée, never. She does the same thing, she goes to work and comes home. We stay home to ourselves. Before, I'd come home and get a shower and I got to go everywhere, go see everybody, do everything, get drunk, raise hell, drugged up a little bit. Smoke a little marijuana, that's all I ever did, smoke marijuana.

It chills you out, and that's one reason why I smoked it. I was always strung out, I was always high; I couldn't sit somewhere two minutes. I'd have to get up and walk, whatever . . . I smoke a joint I could just chill out.

I seen these little kids the other day, they did something wrong, I don't know exactly what they did wrong, I caught the tail end of it. Their mother yanked 'em up and spanked 'em. One of the little kids looked back at the mother and said, *"I wish I was dead!"* I can't believe that child said that, but the child didn't know what it said. But I met death, I know what death is like, and you don't wish you was dead. I don't care how bad it is, or how mad you are, or how sad you are, or how down you get, you never, ever wish you was dead. I used to have bad days, too. My mind would be running wild sometimes and I'd think, *Damn it, it'd be cheaper if I was dead.* I used to have them negative thoughts like that. But I don't have 'em no more. I never ever say I wish I was dead. I don't even like to hear nobody say that about themselves.

But when that kid said that it really kind of froze me. That kid don't really know what it said to its mama, and the mama didn't know either, really. She didn't get excited or nothing, you know?

If that'd been my child I'd have said, "Look here, you don't wish you was dead, and I don't wish you was dead either." It was like she didn't hear it, the mother acted like she just didn't hear it. Me myself, I'd have grabbed that kid up and talked with that kid. Tried to smooth this thing over. But the kid didn't know what it said because it's young, and the mother didn't realize what the kid said because she didn't acknowledge. If she'd have been where I'm at she'd have grabbed that kid up and tried to talk to that kid, like, "What you did was wrong, and I didn't spank you because I don't love you, or I hate you or something, I spanked you so you'll be better." But the mother, the kid said he wished he was dead and she left it like that.

That kid hit me at heart, because I met death. I met it head-on. There wasn't a damn thing I could do with it but go with the flow. I went with the flow. I come back out the other end. Why I come out or how I come out, I don't know. But I did. That's all that matters, that's the bottom line.

My whole body looked like a balloon [in the hospital]. I didn't look nothing like me. They showed me some pictures of me and I made them take 'em away. I told them I didn't want to look at them. Like I said, I blocked a lot of stuff out. A lot of things they did to me I don't know they did to me because I didn't want to know. My mind's real strong. It's like a light switch—I could turn it on, I could turn it off.

I had a boy that got shot just like I did, except he got shot with a smaller gun caliber. His name was Randy, Randy Jones. They put us in the room, he got shot the same night. They operated on him sometime that morning, they operated on me sometime that morning, they brung us out both about the same time. They kept us in intensive care for weeks and weeks and weeks. I mean, we stayed in there a long time, side by side, but we knew we were both in there. And they ended up putting us in a room together after we got out of intensive care.

He was up, he was walking around, he was doing great. They didn't know when I was gonna walk if I *ever* walked. Or if I was even going to make it. I don't remember all this in this time, but the doctors gave my parents nine out of ten I wasn't going to make it. I'd look at that boy walking and stuff there, he'd lost the same amount of everything I did. Everything I lost he lost. Identical. Only thing was the bullet was a different size, a different type. He was up walking around and he was doing good, terrific.

Lately I started remembering stuff like that, because for a long time I didn't. And he was encouraging me to get better. I knew he was telling me something but I couldn't make it out, I was just in a state of mind that, I was out of it. The light was on but nobody was home. He was trying to encourage me to pick myself up. He was getting along real good, I mean super good.

So a couple weeks went by. He was talking to me one day, and there was nobody in the room but me and him. He said, "Randy, I don't want to live no more." I said, "Randy, you can't say that. Here you are getting up getting around real good, and look at me. I'm surviving off all these machines. You're up walking around. How could you say that, after you've come so far." He said, "I don't want to live no more." I said, "You don't mean that, you can't mean that." He said, "I'm gonna give up."

Seven days later he died.

He was doing terrific. They was amazed at how far he'd come in that short period of time. They said, "Nobody's ever done what this boy here's done." There I was over there like a vegetable, you know. The doctors come in there every day and pat him on the back, and pat themselves on the back saying how good he done. They said ten out of ten of what happened to us dies. There is no survivors. That's what they said. If ten come in here like this, ten dies. If a hundred come in here like this, all hundred dies. I was the only one they said ever made it.

That boy, he just give up, and seven days later he died. He said he wasn't walking no more, and he didn't. He didn't walk another step. Said he was quitting, said he give up, said he been in so much pain he could not tolerate the pain no more, and said, "I quit." That's what he told me.

But he never give no explanation of why he was giving up beside that he had pain and he was tired of the pain. He said he done handled it for three months or whatever it was, and he couldn't handle it no more. I said, "Man, talk about pain, look at me. Look at you, you're way ahead. If I get to

where you're at now, I'll be happy." He had conquered all
that.

*****

Sometimes two or three hours, they get [my pain shot] to
me late. I'm dying. I died. What the hell's wrong with these
damn people? How do they treat me like this? They don't
understand, that's the problem. Because if they did they'd
be breaking their neck to get it there on time.

[Doctors] split humans up all the time, therefore to them
it's nothing; you know, "I do this seven days a week, twenty-
four hours a day. This ain't nothing." But they ain't on the
other end of that stick. They're on the opposite end of the
stick that you're on. You don't know until you get to our end
of the stick what it's like.

It tortures you. It just cuts you down piece by piece . . . I
stayed on all kinds of drugs for fourteen months, constantly.
They even told me, "Randy, you might be hooked on some
of this stuff." I said, "When you all say it's over, it'll be over."
They said, "Randy, you don't understand the way drugs
work." I said, "You don't understand the way Randy works."

I'm in pain, and I said, "I know you all gonna take these
pills away from me directly, these shots. And I can't wait till
y'all do. The only reason I take 'em now is because y'all tell
me to." There was a time I could see that I had to have it,
but that was at an earlier stage. When I got 50 percent better
I didn't need nothing to help but me. I programmed myself
for one thing: getting Randy better. I had one goal, getting
Randy better, and I put that in my mind like a computer
chip. Slipped it in. And that's all I cared about. I didn't care
how bad I felt, and I didn't care about when I was gonna get
better. I just knowed I had to do it. And whatever it took,
that's what I done.

They sent me all these therapy people and stuff, you
know. I said, "Get rid of them suckers. Throwing away my
money. Get *rid* of 'em." My daddy had 'em flown in from
God knows, you name it. All kinds, mind- and body-wise. I

just let 'em all go. I said, "That's a waste of money." I said, "Them people irk my ass. I don't want them sons of bitches around me." And I tell it just like that when they're standing there. I said, "I don't mean to call you sons of bitches; that's just a figure of speech to me. I don't mean to be cussing y'all in no way, shape, or form. I think y'all terrific people and thank God y'all here for people that do need y'all. But I want you to take y'all's time, because you're all trained professionals, and I want you to help somebody that really needs y'all." I said, "I don't need you."

They said, "Mr. Walker, you don't know what you're saying," this and that. I said, "I know what I'm saying. There's somebody out there that you need to be helping and it ain't me." They said, "You can't do it on your own. You need somebody to coach you through this thing here, to get back." I said, "There won't be nobody but me." And I did it all on my own.

Psychiatrists, they sent me them sons of bitches hand over fist. Check me out, find out what makes me tick. Hell, I checked them out and told them what made them tick. That's the truth. . . . My opinion on that is it's just a waste of time and money. That's just my opinion. Sure, some people need somebody to coach 'em along, help 'em get their priorities back straight in their head. And their own minds aren't strong enough to do it. But I don't see a shrink doing it. Those sons of bitches are nutty to begin with, as far as I'm concerned.

I'm a strong enough man, in my head, it don't matter how far I get knocked down, I'll always come back. And I always come back stronger and better. I was paralyzed at seventeen years old. I fell off a house and hit a brick wall three-foot high that bent me over in a U shape, caught me in the back. Broke my back in five places. I was laid up for a year and a half. They said I'd never walk again. They set this surgery thing up for me, fifty-fifty. Fifty percent I would, fifty percent I wouldn't. I said, "Doc, that ain't gonna do it." I was seventeen years old at the time, my mama and daddy was pushing me to go ahead and take this operation. But I wouldn't do it. They said, "What you mean? You got a fifty-fifty chance." I said, "That ain't good enough for me. You just told me if you was cutting on me and you made a mistake that you could paralyze me for life. How about if you make that mistake?"

He said, "Well, if I don't have a chance to put you back together you're going to be like you are all your life." I said, "I'll take that gamble." So I laid up for a year and a half.

My father would come in every morning before he'd go to work, and he'd say a little something to me, to try and encourage me along during the day. He come in there one morning and I said, "Dad, I want to get up." He said, "Son, you can't get up." I said, "Dad, *I want to get up.*" Sure enough, he helped me get out the bed and he was holding me up, and I was leaning against the bed and I had no feeling in my legs whatsoever. When he turned me loose I folded up right there on the floor, I just ate the floor up. He took me back up and put me in the bed and said, "I told you you couldn't get up." Next morning he come in there, talk to me again. I said, "I want to get up," so he got me up. I ate the floor up again. That went on morning after morning. Every once in a while I'd skip a morning, because I was so tired of falling on the floor so damn much, that I'd try to conserve myself and try it again. I kept on doing that, kept on doing that.

All these doctors said, "You're wasting your time, son. You need to have that surgery." I would not do it for hell. I walked. I went back to work doing roofing work all over again, doing ironwork all over again. I was seventeen years old; this boy just started doing ironwork. I'd been doing roofing since I was fourteen. So they said I wouldn't walk and I did.

People play games with their own minds. They don't even know it, but they do. I get up every morning, I'm tired, I feel like I'm pulling a trailerload of wood behind me, like I'm climbing uphill pulling a trailer behind me or something. But I don't let it bother me. I just go on. I can go daylight to dark. I can be up on the roofs driving nails or whatever, fourteen, fourteen and a half hours in a day, that's every day. Some days I'm out there welding. In fact if I wasn't talking to you I'd be up there in the air with them right now this moment.

I feel bad, but I don't tell myself I feel bad. I don't hardly tell nobody else I feel bad. People say, "Randy, how you getting along now? You doing all right or you not doing too good?" *Doing fantastic. I didn't know it could be so sweet.* They say, "You really feel that good, son?" I say, "You see me, don't you? I'm doing everything I ever did before."

If I feel bad I don't let 'em know it. I could tell myself, "Oooh, I'm not gonna make it today," and I would stay home, I wouldn't even try to go out and make it. Just because I told myself I couldn't make it. But I *never* say Randy can't do that. Can't is not in my vocabulary. You can make anything negative you want to, and you can make something negative positive if you want.

I think bad things turn out to be good. Like on this shooting of mine . . . before, I looked at you one way. I look at you a whole different way now. There's a lot of good things. I drank before, I don't drink now. I did drugs before, I don't do drugs now. So how's anything negative come out this situation, I don't understand. I used to run with a pretty rough crowd. I was the type of businessman, I could do my business, and separate it totally and be rowdy, a hoodlum, on the other side at night. In other words, I had this group of people I'd run with, and everybody thought highly of me. Then I'd run with this group of people that were nothing but scum. It's like I was two different people.

I didn't smoke before I got shot and I smoke now. I laid up so long, I looked at all the walls, and the ceiling, seen every crack, hole, dust, whatever was on it. Didn't have nothing to do. Couldn't go outside. I was totally in for thirteen months, I mean totally flat. The only outside I seen was through a window or something. That was about it.

I used to never laugh. I was like a scrooge. People'd even

ask me, "Randy, do you ever smile?" But I do now. I laugh about things, this or that. Even if it ain't funny I can make it funny. Yep, things is different now.

One of Randy Walker's goals was to become a millionaire by age 30, which he did. Roofer, builder, businessman, Randy lives in Walterboro, South Carolina.

▪ DRAGON

The Americans were trying to secure the area. [They] claimed that the Americans were trying to get over to their side. We know that some shots rang out, but mostly what happened was they came and chopped some of the Americans away. The army didn't have any unit too close. Since we were trained in hostility and things like that, they sent seven of us [U.S. Marines] to go and see what we could do with the army. To help them out.

When we got there the shit hit the fan. It was going crazy. All I knew is they had a problem and Americans were hurt. We were sent there as a last resort because they didn't have enough people to get there in time. It was real close. Regular speed over there was thirty miles an hour. We got there in like ten minutes.

When we got there some of them were dead. And there were some still alive, Americans. We came, and we tried to do a thing. I didn't know nothing about firing, I mean, I was trained to do what I was trained to do, but I never thought of actually doing it. It's a different feeling altogether. I was scared. A lot of us were scared. To have the possibility of taking somebody else's life in your mind, it's a different thing altogether. You understand what I'm saying? When you're growing up and playing with guns, and you want to be a cop or a soldier, you think it's fun. But when you see reality in front of you it's not the same. When you see a dead body in front of you, you smell the blood. I think everybody goes through the same thing. No matter what. The unit we were trained in, we learned how to handle twelve-gauge shotguns, Uzis, tear gas . . . we went through all kinds of training.

Even though they trained you to war, trained you to fight, I think the reality of knowing that you were going to blow somebody away, when you see the real thing, I think you'll react the same way I did. Because everybody that was with us was like, "Are you scared? Naw naw naw." And we'd start laughing. Yeah, we were scared.

When we got to where we could see, we were trying to pull the guys away that were still alive. We ended up firing, but we didn't know what we were shooting at.

When I got hit, I didn't know I got hit. I got hit with what they call a twelve-gauge slug. A guy told me that when I got hit [in the right shoulder], he actually saw me fly about three feet up in the air, and then I picked myself up. And I didn't realize that I was hit because of what was going on. When I got hit, I felt like a push, but I thought one of the guys was pushing. But I notice now, when I go back over what happened, that my left hand was taking over the job. I'm a righty, but it didn't dawn on me that [my right arm] was wasted.

When we got secured, put everybody in the car, the rest of the army people came in to secure the area, to control it. I was told I was bleeding. And the moment I was told I was bleeding, I was out. I looked down and said, "Oh shit," and that's all I remember.

I woke up in Bethesda three months later.

Bethesda, Maryland hospital. All I remember was my mother was there, and I asked her, "Mom, what are you doing in Korea?" She says, "You're not in Korea; you're in the United States of America." They showed me a mirror, my beard was long. They told me I was away for three months, in a coma.

[The Koreans] used AK-47s. You'd be surprised what the Orientals used for weapons. There are some parts, I think a good example would be the Philippines, they got a mixture of weapons. Korea is the same thing. The ones we were helping out, they were using the M16. Some were using the AK-47s from Russia. You cannot say there was a standard weapon that anybody was using. The only ones with a standard weapon was us. The same thing like in Vietnam. When I joined the service I was just in time for the evacuation. Everybody had all kinds of stuff over there. Whatever they found in the street, they picked it up and they used it, that's all.

I don't know how to explain [the coma] to you. When I woke up, it took like three minutes before I spoke to my mom, and said, "What the hell are you doing here?" My mother went through a phase herself, because her son . . . she went through a phase, too. For some reason they didn't tell her for a long time what happened. My mother had no idea. She came to the hospital about two days before I came out of the coma. There was a time when she had no idea what happened.

I guess you never can tell when someboy's going to come out of a coma. They just come out of it. The moment I woke up, they slated me for an operation. They couldn't do this certain operation while I was out. I had some lead still in the artery, and they couldn't go in while I was in the state I was in.

They gave me an operation. I still have a little piece they can't touch. Just recently, about three years ago . . . you got a piece of metal and your body rejects it, it comes up like a pimple. What they do is come in, they slice it, and pop [the metal] out. So they wait till it comes through the skin. My body had rejected, little by little, some of this stuff already. It's weird because the body rejects the metal and it's right under your skin; you can see a grayness or whatever.

Then the rejection that you feel afterward from the government. Because what happened to me was, after I came out of the operation, I was no longer [fit for my previous duty]. They told me it was time for me to leave. I picked up my next rank, and they offered me duty as a supply chief. *They wanted me to work in a warehouse!* I couldn't do that. The government rejected me, that's how I felt. Like I wasn't good enough to work for the government no more.

I was going to therapy, and at the same time I was going to a shrink. The therapy lasted about seven months, and the shrink was about six months. The shrink was to see if I had any remorse against anybody. They wanted to see if I was a time bomb. Could this guy blow up at any time?

[The North Koreans] were protecting what they were told to protect. I can't hold it against nobody. But I do hold a lot against the government for how I got treated since I got out.

This is gonna make you laugh. A guy that's a redneck, he's a good friend of mine, he was from the Midwest. When we met the first time he said, "You're a spic, I'm a 'neck; we're not supposed to get along with each other. But we got the same room so we got to get along." He always used to hang around with rednecks. They were always talking about black people, you know how they call us lowlifes or whatever. I became the godfather to his son and daughter. We're the best of friends. He got hurt; he says I got hit because I deflected the bullet from getting him. He got hit, a slice on the arm. Not as bad as I did, he got like a nick.

We were just there to get them out. We weren't there to fight, we were there to get the guys that were still alive. The whole thing was, "Grab the people and get the fuck out of there," put it that way. That's all it was. I was a young man in my twenties. I never thought of taking a human life. I never really wanted to. But to save my ass, at the last minute, I'll do it if I have to. It's not a good feeling. It's different when you see a body in a funeral home, okay, because it's prepared. If you've ever seen bodies in front of you, you smell the blood.

The psychological problem with me was that I was going through rejection. I felt like I wasn't worth anything after that was over. I was planning to make the service a career, but they got me so aggravated. They wanted me to become a warehouse guy. Hey, that's not me.

When I got released from the military, all I got was 10

percent [disability]. If I would have tried to get anything above 25 percent, I couldn't get a real good job, or try to get a job. A lot of these companies, as soon as they hear you're taking a big percentage from the military, they won't hire you, like you must have a very bad problem. You understand?

When I got out, I'll give you a good example of what happens to a military person. I have a black belt, and I teach in Manhattan. I'm in good shape; I could walk for miles. I run three miles almost every morning. On the weekends I run five miles, Saturday and Sunday. I work out, I can break boards with my hands and stuff like that. When I got out of the military I applied for the police department. They said, "We can't hire you because you got a screw and pin in your arm." But I could lift everything, I could do everything. "We won't hire you." You're qualified and they don't want to hire you.

They consider the only ones that are vets are Vietnam vets. Anything that happens after Vietnam, if you get injured or whatever, they cannot declare it as an incident. They cannot declare it as anything for you to claim because of the news media. When this happened, this was in the newspapers for I'd say about a week and a half, and they tried to hush it up quick. The made a lot of people sign papers, documents, if you get caught saying a lot of other things that aren't supposed to be said, you're in prison.

If you ever run into anybody that's been in the military after the Vietnam War—military police, any kind of military— if he was hurt on the job, even though he's hurt, he cannot claim preference for anything . . .

When I got out of the military I had no training at all. The only thing I was trained to do was security and being a bodyguard. Now I'm out looking for a job and nobody wants to hire me. I applied for the police department, applied for corrections—my arm held me back. I went to private companies to work as a security guard—I was too overqualified. The guy told me, "You could take my job."

A friend of mine hooked me up on Wall Street. Two years

after I got out of the service I started working on Wall Street. At that time I was working for $200 a week. Recently I got laid off from Wall Street. I was making $575 a week and I got laid off. I go apply for different jobs. I go apply for a doorman. They told me I wasn't qualified for a doorman. I wasn't experienced; I needed two years' experience. I applied for being a regular porter, cleaning up the place. They told me I needed two years' experience.

I got a high school diploma. I go to school to become an investigator. After I get out of the school at the top of my class, I find out the school was phony. So what I'm doing is I'm doing it on my own.

I'm looking for a job, I'm looking for a permanent job, I don't care what it is. Driver, cleaning, whatever it is, $200 a week to start, I'll take it. I need something permanent. A lot of people say you're not qualified. I put in six years in the service. What good is it for a person to be in the service, get hurt, get shot for their country, and he's not qualified for anything else because he doesn't have experience? What is it worth to protect your country? That's my opinion.

Fully recovered from the slug he took in Korea, the Dragon lives in the Bronx, New York.

■ JOE WENTZ

Sixty-nine, toward the end of summer. Almost fall. We just had long-sleeved shirts on. We were coming out of my buddy's house, turned the corner to go up the alleyway. Three guys come out of nowhere saying, "Hey, gimme a quarter."

I stopped and looked at him. I laughed. "Right, get a life," that kind of stuff. And we got in a fight. I mean, if he would have pulled the gun at first maybe it wouldn't have gone down like that. But we got in a fight with 'em, and the guy with the gun was just standing there. Three guys against us. To me it was one on one. So we jump on these other guys and the guy with the gun was more in the background. When I looked at him and said, "Well, you got something to say, man?" That's when he pulled a gun on me and shot.

When he shot it sounded like a tear gas gun going off. Little pops. I said, "What," because I didn't feel the bullet. I didn't know I was even shot. We got in a little bit more scuffle and he ran up the street. I was standing there for a minute and said, "Boy, I feel tired, man." I leaned against a car and went to scratch my nose. And out of the corner of my eye, man, I seen this fountain of blood just shooting out. This is where the bullet went in, left hand [near the base of the thumb] and came out here. I saw the blood coming out of there, it was a steady stream. I said, "Oh man, he really did shoot me."

So we go up to my buddy's house, I'm in his bathroom

now, and my face is all covered with blood. His mom comes up and she falls out like a log because she sees blood all over my face. So I'm taking my shirt off. My shirt's all soaking wet. It's a good bit of bleeding for a little wound. Then I looked down and it was bleeding like that, and I said, "Well shit, the guy got me two times."

What happened was, when he shot me in this hand, the bullet ricocheted off the wall, came back through my arm, my shirt was hanging open, and it came across my shirt. Left hand, upper right arm, and across my shirt. Same bullet. The way it went off, I thought I got shot two times, but the way it came across my shirt I couldn't see how it would have gone that way if it wasn't a ricochet. As far as I know it was a ricochet. The doctors tell me there's a piece of lead still in there that they couldn't get out. They didn't want to bother with it.

Oh yeah, I went to the hospital. They asked who did it to me, and I said, "Just some guy." I never seen him again in my life. Just one of them things. They wrote it down as unsolved, you know?

Over a quarter. That's all it was, a quarter, a lousy little twenty-five cents. He wanted to borrow a quarter. And I wasn't giving him no quarter. They were black guys, and we don't give no money to black guys. I was drinking. One thing led to another, mouth battle, and *wop*, we got into a fight and then here it is, pop pop.

Twenty-five [caliber], that's what it was, a .25. I thought it was a .22, but they told me it was a .25.

[On Joe's chest is a long, curved scar.] That was in a fight, and that guy, I never even seen it coming. It must have been a razor blade,'cause I'd have seen a knife. Just *fssst*, like that, and I was beating on him some more. . . . Then it got broken up and we walked away, and, "*Holy shit, man,*" I said, "*What the fuck?*" We were in a car by then, and we went to my friend's farm. You know how when a cow gets cut? On a farm when a cow gets cut they take this salve-type stuff, and they clean the wound off and they put the salve on. And that's it. That's all we did to this, and that's how it healed. That happened back in '68. I think it healed pretty good for not going to a doctor and getting no shots or nothing.

I grew up in the city, Harrisburg. That's where [the shooting] happened at. About, let's see, four, five . . . eight blocks over. That's where it happened.

A man of many talents, Joe Wentz lives in Harrisburg, Pennsylvania. Just before this interview a motorcycle wreck smashed up his right hand and put him out of work for a while.

■ JIMMY THE GREEK

I've been through so many things personally. The operations alone from the incident, not just getting shot once. I got hit more than one time, then I got bayonetted on top of that. That was the least of the wounds; when I got bayonetted, they just jabbed me like, to see if I'd move. If I moved, then I'd probably get tortured, SOL, shit out of luck. I'd be dead right now.

I think it was harder for me to get rehabilitated after the shooting than anything else. One day for the shooting, right? And I'm still going through rehabilitation even today from wounds that I received in 1966. Some people got over it right away, you know? Got over the shooting. I still get flashbacks like it was yesterday, I still think I'm in it. Sometimes I crack up and start crying, I remember the guys dying all around me.

I can remember myself laying in the hospital, three months after being wounded, staying in the hospital and inhaling the blood. That's how much blood was spilled on the ground in Ia Drang Valley, there was so much blood that it was actually worse than walking into a slaughterhouse. I used to work in a slaughterhouse on the waterfront in Manhattan, downtown in the city, killing pigs. If you think that was bad, it was nothing. This was an outright slaughter when I was there in '65. I think the fight started November 15 or something like that.

Ia Drang Valley. I was stationed at Ankhe, Pleiku, Pleime,

right down in that area with the 1st Cav. I was with an advance party, to lay out the area for the military to go over there in the beginning. That was the beginning of the war, actually, the first real conflict we had, when we really engaged with the enemy. I felt sorry for the guys that were with me. I myself didn't care, really, in one respect. Like I didn't think of getting killed, it didn't bother me. But I was thinking of the kids around me and how young they were. I had already been in Korea.

Like I said, I'm not finished being rehabilitated after all these years. I remember when they were amputating my leg. I'd already had my leg on for a year and they already did I don't know how many operations on it. This time they were going to amputate my leg, it was like my second year in there. It was on my birthday, May 15. Well, I woke up in the OR, the anesthesiologist must have fucked up or something 'cause he didn't give me enough whatever. I woke up, then they put me under again. I remember going to sleep again like, I went out. After that, though, I actually remember myself above the table, looking down at the doctors and everybody and seeing my own body—*me*, seeing *me*—down on the table. I can swear to that to the Lord.

A feeling did come to me, that did say "Go back," like come back into my body. Something said, "Go back." So at that point I must have passed away and come back. I remember that like yesterday. I was looking at them sawing my leg off just like when I was a butcher in a butcher shop—actually seen 'em saw my leg off with a regular saw. Cutting on the bone. Just like that, sawing the femur. I even asked them for my tattoo that I had on my leg and they wouldn't give it back to me. I figured they could cut my skin off and put it in formaldehyde or something, but they wouldn't give me it. Said it was government property. That's exactly what they said. They probably used the goddamn leg to experiment for a bunch of young doctors or something.

See, the VC overran us. We were so outnumbered that there were only a few of us left, fifteen of us left in our outfit like. The point of it was, we figured, being as we were all going to die, we might as well kill all them at the same time, so we called in direct hits right on us. We had the jets coming in on us, they dropped napalm. I remember I was so close to the napalm it almost killed me, when it dropped it sucked the air out of my body. I couldn't breathe. Then after that the artillery rounds came in. I laid there for a day after I got hit.

*****

Ain't that a motherfucker when they point a gun at you and it looks like a cannon? I had them pointing in my face, the side of my head, front of me. In 'Nam we'd spin the barrels, did everything. Did some sick stuff in 'Nam. Real sick. A lot more than a lot of our country, than a lot of our guys, know. Even some of the guys that were in 'Nam don't know some of the stuff that we did. Secret, secret stuff. Real sickening, too.

It's just like, okay, an old cowboy, a gunfighter or somebody. A professional killer. After a while and after so many killings and all, you stop and you just can't do another shooting. You can be the toughest guy in the world, the fastest gun in the world, and after a while you just want to walk away from it all. What's it all for? Why was it all done, why'd we do all this? Why all the killing, what's it getting us? A body count.

*****

One time a guy pulled a blade on me in a poolroom. I ran a poolroom on 31st Street and Broadway in Astoria. Under the El. And when he pulled his blade I had a big Bowie of mine, I whipped it across. Not the front part, but the back part of it, the top part was razor sharp. So I cut this guy. He was another Greek, and a Greek pulling a knife on a Greek, you're not supposed to do that, it's an understood thing. You're insulting me by pulling a knife, you're a Greek and I'm a Greek. He says, "What does that mean?" I said, *whiiiiisht,* "Don't mean nothing." Because he pulled it first.

I slit him across the shirt, and mind, the knife was so sharp, like a razor, when he bent over the pool table, all of a sudden he was holding his stomach. Because I sliced him, not deep, but enough so he realized he was cut. He was bleeding.

A week later another guy, used to make all kinds of money, you could hit him in the stomach with a baseball bat, anything you could do, kick him in the stomach, hit him with a baseball bat . . . Monk, that was his name. He's living today out on Long Island. Strange. A buddy of mine was in the poolroom, one of my guys, and [Monk] pulls a gun on me. It looked like a cannon, you know? And I was near the telephone, I was on the phone at the same time and I says, "The guy's got a gun on me, man." I didn't realize my buddy had snuck around behind him. There was pillars in the poolroom, steel beams going up, pillars. He snuck around, his name was George, he was about ten feet away from Monk.

He told [Monk] to drop the gun. My buddy pulled a piece. Monk turned around and waved his at my buddy, and my buddy went bang one time, it was a .25, caught him with a round in the neck. He dropped to the ground. The guy that owned the place was a retired detective, so he took care of the incident and all. This guy Monk is walking around with a round in his neck right now. Small caliber, they can't get it out.

Jimmy the Greek was hit with bullets and artillery. The back of his thigh, as he described it, "was scooped out clean like an eaten watermelon."

▪ ROLAND

At that time, when that happened, I think I was about twenty-two. Right now I'm thirty-eight. How many is that, about sixteen years? How it happened, it was over a bum drug deal. I had a gun too, and it was either him or me.

Somehow, when we was coming towards each other somebody jumped in front of me and said, "No, you can't do it like that." You're talking about when you're getting ready to do something to somebody in that range all that adrenaline pumping up in you, pumping up in you, and the moment that guy jumped in front of me and said you can't do it like that, all that adrenaline was gone. It just oozed out my body. It was gone. So.

We did meet face to face, we stepped off and we was talking about the money situation and this and that and you know, the whole gamut of that thing, but I didn't know he had a shoulder holster with a .32 up under his jacket. See, I had a .38 in my belt waist but he had a .32 in a shoulder holster up under his jacket and I didn't have no idea. The next thing you know we was talking and it was like, the shit was kind of dark but there was some light in there, and if it wasn't a nickel-plated pistol I probably never would have seen it.

The fact that it was a nickel-plated gun, when he grabbed it, I like went to grab the gun in his hand, and at the same time reached for my .38. All this was happening in like, you know, fractions of a second. When I put my hand on my .38

and grabbed the gun in his hand it went off, the gun that he had, and hit me in the elbow. Now that spun me, hit me in my left forearm, so that spun me towards my left because we were face to face, no more than two feet apart from each other. The impact from that bullet spun me, and the gun that I had flew out of my hand and went in the opposite direction. But I could see, while I was falling, him taking aim again.

He fired a second shot which hit me in the neck. It like dazed me or sorta like took me out for a moment or two and I said, "*Oh shit I'm dead.*" I seen myself falling, but by the time I hit the ground I was conscious of where I was at and what happened, you know, it just seemed like that second bullet hit me in the neck and *bow* . . . all I did was like black out for that matter of two seconds when the bullet hit me and me hitting the ground.

It was strange, 'cause when the people came around me I was trying to get up and they was telling me, "No, stay down there, stay down there." One guy thought I was shot in my head so he was kind of nervous 'cause we was pretty good friends and he didn't want me to get up, you know. But I was trying to get up.

So I laid there till the ambulance came and took me to the hospital, and it was strange. I really didn't feel no pain in the neck; I didn't know what the hell happened in my neck. I knew I was hit. But I didn't feel no pain. The pain was more or less in the elbow, 'cause I think the bone was fractured or something. I laid for a good while in this particular hospital, Lincoln—that was the old Lincoln before they finished the new one. I was there for like maybe two hours. I don't know, I really think I lost the concept of time. But it appeared like I was there a long time and they decided that they couldn't keep me there and they had to send me to Jacobi 'cause they didn't have a neurosurgeon. The bullet in the neck was too close to the spine, so they needed a neurosurgeon to case-conference it. And the funny thing about that, I went to Jacobi—I was conscious, I never went out—

and they asked me and I was telling them [about it] and the slang that I used to describe the scene in the street, they thought I was being a comic. But I really wasn't being no comic.

Anyway, I went through some tremendous traumatic experiences with that bullet. I mean, the medical treatment I had to go through seemed worse than taking the two bullets.

When I got up there they was talking about plastic surgery on my face because my face had gotten scarred up, but I never did get no plastic surgery. So what happened was, I waited. Had to go through a period of time where—okay, when I first got there they put fuckin' needles in my head on both sides. I had to have traction in the head with a weight down the back.

Did I curse them out. I mean, that's all I could do to release the pain and the anger. I know they was trying to help me, but I called them all kinds of names. I couldn't help it. Then I went upstairs, I guess, and I think they operated on the elbow first. But they had the case conference, how the hell they was gonna get that bullet out of my neck. They decided if they leave it in it's gonna move, so we might as well take it out. And they took it out.

They took it out, and laying across from me was a guy that had the same type of wound, and he was paralyzed from the neck down. But he got hit with a .38. They was telling me I was pretty goddamn lucky that it was a .32 rather than anything bigger.

I guess I did go through a lot of traumatic experience in the hospital 'cause they was giving me a lot of antibiotics and other medications. And with this particular type of wound I was not supposed to sleep. That was the deal, I wasn't supposed to sleep. What have we got there, the thalamus and the hypothalamus and all of that, all that controls our breathing mechanisms and all that sort of shit back there.

I guess I really am fortunate to be alive, too. I guess I really am. Because with all the medication they had given me and not allowing me to sleep, eventually, I did fall asleep.

Fell asleep, and I guess that's what you call code blue. They come running and have to hit you with the shock to stimulate your heart, to get your heart moving again. Because they had all those machines on me, I guess when the machines went dead they knew I was dying.

But fortunately—talk about fortunate, that's really, really fuckin' fortunate. It's like a matter of seconds before you get brain dead, after the oxygen stops going to the brain.

They did what they was supposed to do, reviving me and all that good shit. Then the next thing I know I'm in the operating room again, and I asked them, "What the hell am I doing here?" They explained, "Well, you fell asleep. Now we gotta operate on you again and we gotta give you a trache so you can breathe." So now I had to have a tracheotomy so I could breathe, which was another traumatic experience. We breathe subconsciously, we do this, it's just a normal thing. But when you really have to concentrate on your breathing, in-out, in-out, it's not as easy as it appears to be. I got scared a couple times when I lost the rhythm.

I lost the rhythm and now I'm trying to catch that rhythm back again, back and forth. That shit is really scary. Then I realized the beauty of my doctors. I had a good doctor in the chief neurosurgeon at Jacobi. The job he did—everybody that worked with me personally, worked with me or on me medically, was fucking great. *Fucking great.* I gotta say that the staff there took care of me, they was great. They did what they had to do, even though at times, some of the things . . . you know, they come and take blood, they don't take it from my veins, they go into my fuckin' arteries, the groin, right by the wrists right here. I mean like, the shit was so fuckin' painful I gotta curse 'em out, "*What the fuck are you doing to me?*" But they knew what they was doing.

Then it had a mental effect on me also. With the medication and not getting the sleep I started hallucinating. Drastic hallucinations. We're talking about somebody that grew up in the Bronx and knows the Bronx. I'm in Jacobi Hospital, this incident happened around 161st Street and Trinity Avenue. I think the hospital's on Caldwell Avenue, which is around the corner, and there's no hospital there at all. I tell the doctors and the nurses that the guy's outside the windowsill and he's coming to get me. So that's like really, really hallucinating, to the point where they had to give me a brain scan, call a psychiatrist in, ask me if I ever took any hallucinogenic drugs. I told 'em, "No, I never took none before, I'm all right." They called my family in. But it was that medication and the sleep. When you got to try to not sleep for not just hours but days, when you're having all sorts of medication pumped into your body, it can do a hell of a job to you.

Then, my doctor told me when I was leaving to not think about some of the things I had experienced in the hospital. 'Cause I went through a hell of a lot. So don't think about it 'cause you got to give it time and it'll wear off. I went through a hell of a lot in there. Like when I first came home from the hospital I was hearing gunshots at night, you know. I never heard 'em in the hospital, but I was like reliving that episode. It was hell.

When I look back on it now, all I can say is I was lucky. Sometimes I get a little funny feeling in my little finger to the back of my forearm there where the scar is. I've adjusted to whatever minor medical difficulty this might cause. Only sometimes it causes a stiffness in the neck, and I attribute that to the operation and the bullet. Sometimes I'll turn my neck and that shit'll cramp up on me. You know what a cramp in the neck is like. Just like if I gotta stretch it or something, I turn it and say, "Uh-oh, can't turn it too fast." So I have to adjust myself to certain things. Sometimes even the shoulder here, I think the whole muscle part up here might have been affected. No, I don't have no weather damages. It don't bother me when it rains.

I didn't have to worry about him. Somebody else took care of him, see, 'cause he went around as a tough guy and somebody else caught up with him. We seen each other, see, we knew each other. I would have done what I needed to do to protect myself, or else that shooting would never have occurred like it did. I was totally off guard. If it was to happen again it would be him, not me. Definitely. See, we knew each other quite well, and I didn't think it would have to come down to that. I was willing to protect myself, but I let my guard down and got shot up. Point-blank.

He really liked that particular style of living, thought he was tough, and he owned a little after-hours club. Next thing I know he got in a beef with somebody at the club, got shot. And this was maybe two or three years after our altercation. So I guess you could say I really didn't have to worry about that, 'cause eventually somebody's going to serve him. You can't live like that continuously without putting yourself on the firing line.

One thing I'm glad about: I don't live like that no more. That should keep me outside that realm. Hopefully.

People ask me about this [scar] and I say it was an operation. 'Cause when you do tell people, "Well, I got shot," it's like, "Wow." It really sets you apart. Hopefully, I don't encounter them situations. I don't live like that, you know? Right now I'm even afraid to pick up a gun. I lived that lifestyle for so long that, let's say I have some sort of spirituality within myself and I do believe—let's say I have certain metaphoric beliefs. And that gun, being that I'm not a peace officer and using it in the line of duty, if I pick it up, that might bring some of the negativity towards me that's out there. And then, yeah, I will be forced to use it. 'Cause I'm gonna use it. That's why I have it, to use it. And yeah, the thought of owning a gun has been swinging back and forth like a pendulum in my head, because you don't know what's likely to happen out there.

I'm saying, "Wow, I don't want to do that, I don't want to make that move." Why else would you buy a gun if you're not a gun collector? See, I couldn't afford to get arrested with a gun. If I got arrested with a gun it'd be a game of cards for a while. And then who knows, I might not be able to survive the madness in [prison], you know, so I have to deal with things the best way I know how.

Mine was sixteen years ago, and after a while it just becomes something that happened. You might have physical marks to always remind you. It serves its purpose. I mean, I'm just trying not to live the previous life-style of doing damage, doing harm, and then just saying the hell with it altogether. Because hey, you can't live like that. You can't kill up the whole world. Somebody steps on your toes, you don't take out the elephant gun and blast 'em. You know, I'm working with a lot of jerks and I gotta deal with it like that. And some of them do things and you say, "Wow, I wanna blow his fuckin' head off." But you can't respond in that manner.

Like I was saying, in the years since that guy got knocked off, my ego don't feel as damaged as if he was still running around. People ask me what happened sometimes. I give it to 'em in a vague manner, not that somebody else knocked him off, but hey, well, he ain't around no more. Which he ain't. So that's an open end, you know? So my ego don't fuck with me like, "Yeah, that guy did it and you didn't get him back." Because I don't have to deal with that. He's gone. Somebody else did it. You can't just do as you please out here in this society, not forever.

Physical recovery. I went to physical therapy, basically for the elbow. I had to get the strength back in the hand, be able to make a fist. They had to straighten out the elbow. The neck was basically . . . a bone was fractured in the neck 'cause I had a brace on there, but I didn't have to exercise the neck.

I probably went for like three months. They were surprised. I was in and out of the hospital in less than a month; the whole recovery process was quick. Made me feel good. Especially when I was able to leave and get out of there after being cooped up in the hospital. It was hot; it happened during the warm months, you know.

I used to go to my physical therapy like I was supposed to, but it was sort of painful, straightening out that elbow, getting it to the full extension that it could go. Slightly painful. 'Cause I guess for like three weeks, damn near a month, it was up at that 45-degree angle. I just had to work it out slowly. I was working with it there a couple of times, and you know when you do something and it becomes so fuckin' frustrating and tiresome you just want to say, "Fuck it"? I felt like that a couple of times. It reminded me of when I was going to school and we had to do a phonetic exam. You know phonetics? I had no fuckin' concept of phonetics and I wanted to cry, "*What the fuck is this?*" Same thing I got with that, you know, 'cause there was something I was supposed to be doing and I just wasn't able to grab hold and do it right.

I didn't like everything, but I had to have confidence that what they were doing was the right thing. I was on the bed in the nude, an *ice* bed. Anytime they detected I had a fever? That was torture. They turn on that fuckin' thing and the whole bed is *zip*, ice cold. I used to beg nurses to turn it off. They come by and look all sympathetic and stuff and they'd say, "Can't; you got a fever." This was in the intensive care ward. A lot of 'em, they wanted to do whatever they could.

A couple of them went out of their way to do some things for me and their supervisors came down on them real hard. And at that time I couldn't talk, either. One nurse called me a dummy. I was trying to write something on a clipboard. You know it's hell writing upside down on a bed, you're flat on your back, you can't raise up, and you gotta write. It's tiresome. And it becomes scribble-scrabble to some extent. She called me a dummy and I threw the clipboard at her. And she tried to physically harm me.

Yeah. I had to kick at her. She was trying to hit me. I threw the clipboard at her. I remember that.

Roland lives and works in Manhattan.

■ LAURA NEWMAN

Mine was bad luck, a combination of a small amount of obliviousness and 90 percent being in the wrong place. It was Williamsburg [Brooklyn] right in front of my studio. Driggs and Grand. It's not a bad area, really, it's a borderline area. A lot of artists have moved in but there's also a lot of drugs.

It was eight o'clock at night or so, and I was leaving the studio to come home. I don't live out there, I just work there. I was crossing the street on the way to the subway and I noticed a crowd of people, but there wasn't anything unusual about that. About midway across the street I thought I stepped on a firecracker. Then I heard someone say that I'd been shot.

A drug dealer was trying to shoot another drug dealer. It went in one side of my knee and out the other. I was basically very lucky. It was a .22, small caliber. Someone had seen it from above and they thought I was getting a lot of attention for a sprained ankle.

Immediately a million people called ambulances. Someone even called and said a policeman had been shot, so there were instantly a couple of ambulances. I guess the bad thing is that in New York people have to go to the nearest hospital.

[Woodhull Hospital] is a hellhole, basically. It's horrible. While we were there a nurse was desperately trying to find some ice for somebody whose head was bleeding. She ended up just filling a plastic bag with cold water. Someone was smoking crack in the bathroom. It was pretty awful. So the woman who was seeing me said, "What I would advise you to do is check out against doctor's orders and take the IV and just go to Bellevue." So we did that.

I got treated [at Woodhull] to the point where they did an X-ray. There was some concern that there was internal bleeding, but it didn't seem likely. They didn't have the equipment to tell, really. They knew that there was nerve damage, but they couldn't tell how severe it was. It was very good advice.

It was a very frightening experience. I never imagined that a place like [Woodhull] existed. You have the idea in the back of your mind that poor people have Medicare, so they get good medical aid, and it's disturbing when you realize they get really shitty aid. Bellevue has a great emergency room, but the clinic is mostly poor people, and it's mostly black and Hispanic, and it's dreadful. There are a lot of people with broken legs and there aren't any chairs to sit down on. It's pretty awful.

But at Bellevue I got good care initially. I was lucky. [The bullet] chipped the bone but it basically went in one side and out the other side. It was pretty clean. It hit the sheath of the nerve, so it didn't actually sever the nerve. That was the lucky part, because the sheath grows back faster than the nerve body. By November there was movement again. There wasn't full movement, but I could control it. From April, April 21st. I did physical therapy over the summer; by the end of the summer, really, there was more response. I felt like there was response but I was afraid to believe that it was actually coming back. One thing they told me was that the nerves come back but the muscles haven't been used for a long time, so it takes them a long time.

I was there [Bellevue] for about five days. No one really knew how severe it was. I was on crutches for eight weeks, but that's because the bone was chipped. I mean, I was unlucky to get shot in the first place—everyone says it would have been much luckier if the bullet had gone between my legs. But other than that I was extremely lucky. That kind of nerve damage, two weeks, three weeks from when I got shot it was starting to grow back. And then once it was over I went back to the studio. Other than being on crutches I didn't feel traumatized by it. I've had a lot of death and near-death around me, and it was terrible, but I didn't feel that traumatized.

I was in a drop-foot brace until March 1st. Pretty recently. I was able to start weaning myself away in November, December, but every time I would not wear it my back would go out. That was really much more severe than the leg problems because I couldn't function. I went hiking last summer and I wore a brace and shorts and I was fine. I don't know what it was, it could have been anything. Backs are weird things . . . it was just very disturbing because I wanted to get rid of the brace and every time I'd take it off it would mess up my back.

I remember getting the X-rays [at Woodhull Hospital] and shaking like a leaf because I was in physical shock and I couldn't stop shaking and the X-ray technician was screaming at me to stop shaking so she could get a good picture. It was a horrible place. Bellevue was great; it's one of the best trauma centers in the country.

I've been affected by it, but I don't believe I've been traumatized by it. A very good friend of mine died a couple weeks ago. One of the things that I think made him die was, he had Hodgkin's disease, and he was always a very stubborn person. I'd always felt that his stubborness was a quality that was a minor irritation. You know how you assign people characteristics that kind of make you throw your hands up and laugh. And I was thinking that these minor characteristics can kill you. Like my obliviousness. Someone else walking across the street probably would have noticed the people and stayed on the other side of the street. It's a minor fault, like absentmindedness. Something you would never put on your list of bad faults. It's a silly, minor thing. Anyway, it's something to watch out for. And on the other hand, maybe I couldn't have avoided it. And maybe if I'd tried to avoid it instead of going through my knee it would have gone through my head.

I love my studio there. That's a place I really care about. I own it and I've worked really hard to make it nice and I don't want to have to move. It's bad enough someone shot me and put me through all this hell . . .

[Laura later found out that the police knew who shot her.] His name is Reuben and he lives on South Second. But they don't have enough witnesses to do anything about it. Everyone's terrified of the crack dealers. No one will testify, understandably, even though a lot of people saw what happened.

When he shot me he was trying to shoot someone else and he managed to graze the forehead of the other guy. He was in the hospital the same time I was there. But we didn't find out until a lot of friends went to meetings in the neighborhood and at one of the meetings one of the detectives said that. They hadn't been able to get any convictions on either one. I can certainly understand why people didn't want to testify. In that neighborhood I don't know how many people are legal immigrants anyway.

Laura Newman is a painter based in New York City.

■ "New York"

By the time I got to Vietnam it was 1969. There was no
North Vietnamese Army. Nothing organized. It was just
guerrillas, the VC. So there was no real head-to-head battle,
troops-to-troops. It was all sniping, a quick little skirmish
with two or three of them. That was basically it; we were just
patrolling everywhere. The marines stayed out in the field,
and I was a marine. What we did was, we just went within a
certain area, within a few square miles. We just went from
this hilltop to that one, to that one, back to this one, stop in
the middle. Just mix it up in that area.

Whatever fighting I saw, and I saw like three or four en-
gagements, firefights, were not major at all. Most of the guys
were being hurt by booby traps and sniping. There was even
one point where we saw a squad of them about a thousand
meters away, and they saw us, and they went that way and we
went our way. (laughs) We didn't want to run half a mile to
chase these guys, and by the time you call in artillery it takes
twenty minutes and they'll be gone.

They were afraid of us. If they saw us they'd go the other
way. In fact there was an incident on Christmas Eve, which is
when I got hit. We went up this hill, which turned into a
mountain. It was so foggy you couldn't see your hand if you
stretched your arm out in front of your face. Literally that
foggy. We were walking fairly close, the entire company, up
the mountain. We had to get on top by nightfall. Which I

didn't understand because you couldn't see anyway. You could just about make out the form in front of you.

The point guy walked up on two Vietnamese eating. They were cooking something. You couldn't even smell it, that's how thick the fog was. We walked right into them. He loaded up, and they grabbed their shit and took off. He was firing into the fog.

Two things that surprised me about war. One was the noise, and the other was the smoke. After the first shot, you can't hear anything. So you can't bark commands like they do in the movies. Everybody's got to know their job and do it. And two, you can just about see. They use the cheapest powder to make military ammunition and explosives. Anything like a hand grenade goes off, and you can't see for a few minutes. Just from a hand grenade, so you can imagine. Plus, the distance. You're looking twenty, thirty feet away, and you throw a grenade and it blows up, you've got a little cloud of smoke there for a while, so you don't know if the guy ran away or you got him or what. It was a round [grenade]. We called them baseballs. There was a military term for it. Everything has an M number, or a P or whatever. The new hand grenade is round, it's not like World War II . . . they figured Americans were more adept at throwing a round thing like a baseball. More guys had thrown them more accurately than just an open-palm heave, so they came up with this baseball thing. I don't know, I didn't really see a difference. You don't throw that many anyway. Especially not in this kind of thing. This is spray the area, this is assault weapons.

My guys opened up against one guy who was running away from us. We started to chase him and I said, "Hold it." We had all our equipment and shit, it's a hundred and thirty degrees, and the guy's running away from us. Everybody's firing, eight guys, including bloop—that's the rifle grenade, M-79 grenade launcher. It's just a tube with a stock . . .

He was firing, and he hit real close to the guy, and the guy blew up into the air, fell down, and we're all shooting away

at him, he was well within range. He gets up and keeps going. He shoots him again. There's an explosion, the guy gets
up and keeps going. I said, "Forget it, hold your fire, no
good. If he can survive two grenades and all this fire, let
him go."

Anyway, Christmas morning we're walking up this hill,
and it turns out that it's a riverbank that's dried up, a
riverbed. We're on one side of it, and it goes down to where
the river had been. We just happened to be on this side. I've
got the radio in the first squad, and the whole company is
behind us. I'm like the fifth man back out of a hundred and
fifty guys. And my radio's not working. We couldn't figure it
out, the batteries or what. Put new batteries in and it still
didn't work. So I'm carrying this piece of junk for nothing,
virtually, and it weighs twenty-five pounds, in addition to
whatever else you carry. I used to carry as much as I could. I
carried about thirty magazines, ten grenades. I didn't want
anyone to get the best of me. I had a pistol and an M16. Plus
your canteens, food if you have any, and whatever else. It's a
lot, you're carrying anywhere from fifty to seventy-five
pounds. Plus I'm carrying the radio, that's another twenty-
five, plus the batteries are two pounds apiece. So whenever
they drop you new batteries they drop you like ten of them,
so you're carrying an additional twenty pounds around.

It's like an upgrade, but there's a slope on one side so
we're watching our footing because it's the sloppy season,
you know, it's monsoon season, the rainy season. And the
weather clears a little bit, we're up high enough to where
the fog is thinning out.

I see the point man walking backwards toward me, stopping and whispering something at each guy, and he gets to
me and he says, "Fall down." By the time he got to the ninth
or tenth guy, the shit hit the fan. Right opposite us was a
bunker. We later found out it was a whole network of tun-
nels under this hill, and it was like the supply station for
them in the side of this mountain. Turns out it was a mountain and not a hill, it was over three thousand feet up.

We didn't see it. Apparently they saw us, or heard us, because we were clanking a lot, you know. When the guy said fall down I just let the weight of the radio and all my stuff just carry me. I just fell back, onto the side of this mountain.

They were shooting what sounded like a machine gun at us, and other little pops and crackles, you couldn't really tell what kind of weapons. There is a definite difference between the AK-47 and the M16 in sound. You can tell which of those two weapons is firing. The AK-47 makes a crack, and the M16 makes a pop. There's a definite distinction, so you can tell what weapon's going off most of the time. These guys—like I said, there was no organized army left, these guys were all peasants. They threw whatever they had at us.

In fact, I'm sitting there, there's a guy in front of me, we're facing each other, and we light up to have a smoke. We figure there's enough fog they can't see us smoking. I forgot I had the radio. I had the whip antenna, which is ten-feet high, because we were in a valley going up. I forgot all about it, and we're sitting there having a smoke, I'll never forget it, and a jar of Maxwell House instant coffee, without the labels—I could tell it was Maxwell House because the lid had all the little white stars on the red background; today it's just one big one, but back then they used to have a bunch of stars all over the top—it was a small size, eight ounces? It was a Chinese—we called 'em Chi Coms, Chinese Communists—grenade. A homemade hand grenade. That's why they told us to break up cans and bottles and don't throw anything away whole.

So this thing comes in and lands right between him and me, and it sits there. We both knew what it was. We both just covered up. He went into a fetal position and I just froze. I just stared at it and wondered when it was going to go off. It blew, and it blew straight up. The glass and everything blew straight up. We didn't get a scratch, either of us. They fill 'em with nails, broken glass, anything they can get.

So everything calms down, we're walking further, we go and count them, and we had another problem. Same situation as the riverbank, and rifle fire breaks out so we all get down. I was hit in the first volley, before I fell down, only I didn't know it. I was hit in the middle of my shin, just to the inside of the bone. Just missed the bone, so I didn't feel anything. It had to be a small-caliber bullet because it didn't go in that far. The squid just picked it out. The corpsman. The marines don't have medical, it's all navy. We had a guy that joined the navy to get out of fighting. They made him a corpsman and he's there traveling around with the combat troops. We used to call 'em squids. There's a nickname for everything in the service.

So, the guy behind me says to me, you were hit, and points to my leg. What do you mean I was hit? There was no blood or anything. There was a little hole in my trousers, so I rolled it up and sure enough, there's a little piece of metal sticking out. It was like a .22 or a .25. Whatever they had they threw at you. The bombs that didn't go off when we used to bomb from the planes, they would build catapults and throw them at our positions. They were called "lob bombs." Five-hundred-pound bomb coming in at you . . . it worked. Whatever.

The guy said to me, "You're shot." I tell the corpsman, "I want to check and make sure." He checks it out and picks out the little piece of lead. But he didn't put any monkey blood on there: Mercurochrome or iodine, any disinfectant. It was red so they called it monkey blood. He didn't put any in there and we didn't bandage it, because it wasn't that bad of a wound. I put a Band-Aid on it, I think, and that was it.

And we went on about the business of being an idiot out in the jungle, in the middle of nowhere at Christmastime. We got to the place, at the top of the hill now, and we got an urgent message on the radio—my radio was working now, this is Christmas Eve—that the Bob Hope troupe has landed safely in Da Nang. That's the end of the message. That's the message. We shouldn't worry about the Bob Hope troupe.

They knew, I guess it was in '65 when the marines finally went in in strength, that you don't fuck with Americans on their holidays. And after the first time that they did, they never did it again. They lost a big offensive on a Christmas Eve or a Christmas Day. They got the shit kicked out of them, which they usually did anyway, but after that they wouldn't do anything else at Christmas.

So here it is, my turn at Christmas Eve, 1969. We get a call that everybody should face one direction. North, I believe. We were south of Da Nang, ten or twenty miles south, and they're calling all the positions, all the people out in the bush, to face north at midnight.

We're all wondering, all right, get more guys on this side, set up the machine guns facing this way. What's coming? Precisely at midnight they shot up these mortars into the shape of a Christmas tree, red and green ones. Mortars hang there for a while and kind of drift down. So everybody's looking north thinking that's where the attack's going to come from and this tree goes up in the sky.

So okay, it's Christmas Day and they fly out a hot meal, which I thought was ridiculous. Guys are coming off the helicopters, we're expecting replacements and supplies, and these guys are coming off with these huge vats full of chickens, turkeys, something, and they gave us a hot meal. And mail. They dropped the mail to us. We hadn't had mail in two or three months because they didn't want to waste the good flying time. When the weather clears up they want to resupply and get men in and out rather than mail drops. I guess they held it to make sure everybody got something. And I got a carton of cigarettes, Marlboro. That was the king over there, Marlboro. I kept two packs for myself and the rest were gone like that. I made sure I gave one to the lieutenant.

So now it's the 26th, the day after. I'm feeling hot. I'm burning up. Then I'll start shivering, like cold, then hot, then cold. So they tell me it could be malaria, those are the symptoms for malaria. I had to go out on patrol, my squad. I get up and my leg hurts. From the knee down it's like pain. It's like a thousand needles or nails or something. A *pain* pain. I was feeling hot, in my head, and that was just pain, like somebody was ripping it up with knives. I said, "Holy shit," and I'm using my rifle as a crutch. I'm having trouble keeping up.

I said, "This is no good." It's gotta be something to do with that fucking bullet. So we get back into the rear area, the encampment, and I said to the corpsman, "Doc"—we used to call him Doc. We'd call a doctor Doctor and the corpsman Doc. You don't call a surgeon Doc, you call him Doctor or his rank. "Doc, something's wrong with my leg. I'm hot, cold." He said, "There's nothing wrong with your leg." He looks at it, and there's nothing there. Just a funny kind of scratch, like you get from a cat. I look at it and say, "Doc, it's the leg." He says, "No, no, no, you're hot and cold," took my temperature, and he says, "You've got malaria." So he made me sleep without my shirt that night, outside. I couldn't get into a tent or anything. It drops about fifty degrees, so you feel the cold. It goes from about a hundred and thirty to seventy. Seventy isn't bad, it's nice. But not when it's been a hundred and thirty. And you're wet. And the wind's blowing. So in that sense it's cold.

So I'm sleeping outside, and I'm shivering, and I'm trying to tell them it's not that, it's the weather. But he tags me for malaria. I'm supposed to be shipped out tomorrow for malaria. They put a tag on you somewhere and they write on it what it is. The helicopter comes, I get on it, they took me off to the hospital. They see me limping at the hospital and they realize it's my leg. They had more insight at the hospital; I guess they saw a lot more than the guys in the field. Guys in the field just patch you up immediately as best they can and ship you off. I have a lot of respect for those guys, the navy guys in Da Nang. When the helicopters start coming in they were practically jumping on 'em. Like at the beginning of "M.A.S.H.," they do that.

A captain comes over to see me and I tell him it's my leg, it's not malaria. He takes my boot off, and my leg swells up to twice its size. The boot was holding it. They also took my sock off, and the sock just corrodes right off. Dust. He says, "When was the last time you changed your socks?" *You've gotta change your socks!* The supplies they gave us were shit out there. I said, "Oh, I didn't take any on the last supply." I didn't want to get anybody in trouble.

This guy knew right away, this captain. He calls two corpsmen over. I'm lying in a ward with other guys. He says to the one corpsman, "You hold that shoulder down, you hold that shoulder down, and you hold this leg down, you hold this ankle down." I said, "What's the 'hold him down' stuff?" he says, "This is gonna hurt." No anesthetic, no nothing.

It hurt. What had happened was, it had started to get infected and the infection was making a channel through the leg and into the bone. There was a little channel in the bone. This is in the meat. The meat was getting infected and where it sits against the bone it was eating the bone. They told me afterwards that if I'd gotten there three hours later they would have had to amputate that leg. There would have been nothing they could do to save it.

It was something you get before gangrene. It's the first stage. And that's what I had. When he started to dig—he scraped the infection out—the sheets were soaked. I wasn't wearing a shirt, just pajama pants. I'm holding onto this bed for dear life, this guy is holding me down at all four corners. And he's digging away and scooping away and digging around. It was the most painful thing I ever went through in my life. And after he's all done, I'm lying there soaked, and he takes a piece of gauze, real thin, like a fettucine, and he stuffs it in. Slowly he starts packing it in. See, they wanted it to heal from the inside up. They didn't want it to close over, because the same shit'll happen.

Every day they would change the dressing twice and give me four shots in the stomach. They give you no pain killers, I don't know why. Darvon was the thing. No morphine in the service. Darvon was what it was called. It's a pill, it's available to the public here. But the dosage was like five hundred times what the over-the-counter stuff is. This is for legs blown off in the field, they give you Darvon pills, so you can imagine how powerful it was. I guess they thought the shit was nonaddictive, I don't know. Morphine, you heard horror stories of guys coming home addicted after World War II, vets in the hospital addicted. So they gave us this shit. I didn't get any because I didn't have any wounds that they considered serious. A leg, to me, is serious.

I said to one of the corpsmen one night, "How come I didn't get a Purple Heart for this?" He said, "See that guy over there? He's got no legs. He gets a Purple Heart. You still want a Purple Heart?" I said, "Alright, alright." For twenty-nine days I didn't get out of bed except to go to the bathroom on crutches. The thirtieth day I had to get up and learn how to walk again. Took me almost half a day to practice walking. Your muscles get all soft. But it healed up and they sent me back to what they call light duty, which is like picking up the garbage around the base and this kind of stuff. No combat for a while to make sure it heals.

That's my story. I tell people this story now and they look at me and expect to see my leg all ripped up. But there's just a blemish. You know those things you get from chicken pox? A little thing like that. And I almost lost my leg over this.

If I walk too much . . . if I walk like fifty, sixty blocks, I'll get an ache, a dull ache. But other than that . . .

In Vietnam they called him "New York." An artist, he still lives and works in that city.

■ DETECTIVE SERGEANT MARTIN BARRETT

July 1969. I saw a car parked on Charlotte Place, and it looked shady. I can tell you the license plate today; it was FUB 426. It turned out to be stolen out of Fort Lee at the time of the burglary, but it wasn't reported stolen.

I saw a guy sitting in the car, I didn't think he belonged there. It was on the side of a house. I called for assistance a couple times, and there was no assistance to be had. S_____ was on vacation at the time, there was only four of us working, and the detectives were unavailable. I pulled up beside the car and asked the guy, "What are you doing here," from car to car, and he says, "I'm looking for Woodland Street." Which would make sense, it was a very good answer. If you went straight up you'd go into Palisade Avenue and the next block down would be Woodland. Two blocks down.

I told the guy to stay in the car and I backed my car up. We're supposed to put the lights on the car. I told him to stay in the car. I got out of my car and walked toward him, and as I started walking toward him, he got out. I couldn't shoot the guy for getting out, because maybe he didn't understand me correctly. He just turned around real slowly with the gun by his balls and started shooting. I said, "Holy shit, this guy's trying to kill me." So I started shooting back at him and I ran behind the car and he ran into the woods, and that's the last time I ever saw the guy. He hit me right in the stomach and it came out here [back]. It just missed everything, though. It didn't do anything, didn't hurt. The operation was terrible. I remember I had a raw hamburger that night from the Cliff Deli and I tasted that raw hamburger for a friggin' week.

They never found the gun. They found six or seven guns stolen. The police chief in Fort Lee, Dalton's house, they'd broken in there. They had a .45 in the front seat. But they think it was a .38 [that I got shot with]. They never found the bullet.

It just felt like I got burned with a cigarette; it didn't hurt at all. It went right through. There's a hole here and a hole here. The doctors said it was a centimeter away from any vital organs. I was in there [hospital] for almost a week probably. The operation was ten times worse than the shooting. If they hadn't done nothing it would have been fine. But they said the bullet can go in and go different ways, so they had to do [a full exploratory surgery]. I wish they didn't, but that was definitely what they had to do.

They called in some guy, Doctor B_____. Whether he ever operated on anyone else in his life, I don't know. They don't tell you. The guy in the hospital was very bad, though. I remember, it was some guy who didn't speak English too good, and he was trying to push something in my chest. It's hurting like hell, I don't know what the hell he was trying to do.

I had to yell to Billy to come in there. Turned out the guy was pushing it in the wrong way. I don't know who he was or what the hell it was, but they called the doctor and made him stop. I think they were trying to put a tube in there to keep the lung so it wouldn't collapse. The nurse told me later on that that's what it was. He was doing it the wrong way, though. I didn't know any better. All I knew is that it was hurting like hell and he wasn't getting no place putting it in. He kept trying and trying . . . They probably don't get that many gunshots around here anyway, in our hospitals.

They caught a guy, but it turned out that the DA never prosecuted. They never told me what happened; that was one of my main complaints. I was never advised about what transpired afterward. They dismissed the charges. The prosecutor's office did that themselves. They felt they had a bad case.

I identified the guy, but obviously . . . I saw a black guy. When I went the first time to the grand jury they showed me a lineup of white guys. I said, "I can't pick the guy out, this isn't the lineup that I saw." I know what they gave me, they gave me a lineup of somebody else. Apparently the black guy I saw was with a white guy. The white guy shot a dog in the backyard a couple houses away. So they made a mistake somewhere in the system and showed me the wrong lineup. They did eventually correct it another time, and I had to go back and pick out a black guy.

But obviously that wasn't good enough for the prosecutor's office. The guy's lawyer had some sort of lie detector test that said he was there, but he didn't do the shooting. That's what it turned out to be. Whether I saw the wrong guy and it was somebody behind him in the bushes, I don't know.

That kept me out of the service, actually. I had to go for my draft physical in September. I was still oozing at the time from the operation scars. The doctor there said, "Jesus, forget about it."

I didn't see the gun at all. I more or less got shot before I realized what happened. I don't remember seeing a gun. I might remember seeing a flare, a light, or something like that, it was real dark in the area, but I don't remember seeing anything before that. The guy did it very nonchalantly. I emptied my gun. I didn't realize I shot six shots but I did. The whole area was all woods behind me. They never found any bullets at all. I think they found a bullet a couple years later in a house, but it could have been his bullet.

I wasn't satisfied with the way I was treated by the department afterwards. All of a sudden two days later they put an order up that you will not stop a car unless there's a backup with you. I had called for a backup and there was no backup available at the time. One guy was going for coffee, I know he was at the coffee place, and the two detectives were busy.

So nobody could come down. But the chief must have heard some different information somewhere.

Martin Barrett is with the Englewood Cliffs Police Department, Englewood Cliffs, New Jersey.

▪ STEVE FULLER

My royal derriere. I was living in a squat on Sixth Street between [Avenues] C and D, and I went out one morning walking my dogs. Across the street these kids were doing some kind of drug deal. Next thing I know there's things flying around me, some serious shit. I was just minding my little puppies, you know?

I felt something burn. It knocked me against the wall. I didn't think I was shot, I didn't know what the hell it was. I've had my share of wounds, but I never felt no shit like this. It's like when they give you a needle in the hospital and they tell you to drop your drawers. They never give it to you where the fat is, they always get you right where the bone is, you know?

So I went upstairs and I started feeling wet back here [his ass]. It's a good thing I had on leather jeans, because leather's tough. I went and laid down and had a bottle of Southern Comfort, you know? When I tried to get up I couldn't move. I was sore, stiff. So I made it down to the park and a friend of mine says, Man, you don't look so good." I didn't. I didn't feel good at all. I was sweating.

Then we went on a chase. He put me in his van, and the first idea was to take me to Downtown-Beekman. He's driving like a maniac. I was denying it the whole way, but he knows I'm not well. He's seen the blood all over me. These little side streets in Chinatown, this guy trashed his van. He hit this one car, it was full of Chinese mob or something, they all had little

96

bats and they got out and they're banging on the side of the van, 'cause we sideswiped 'em. So we had to get out of there quick, because he's got an expired license.

To make a long story short, he takes me to St. Vincent's over on the West Side. They take me to triage and ask what's the problem. I said, "Here's the problem." They cut everything off me in thirty seconds, and the next thing I know I have a million cops: cops from the Ninth Precinct, cops from the Fifth Precinct, detectives from the Sixth Precinct. They wanted me to pick somebody out of a lineup and all this shit. I said, "You guys don't understand. I gotta live in this fucking hellhole. I can't go around pointing people out. I was just at the wrong place at the wrong time." They said, "We don't care about that."

Now, every time I walk around the neighborhood people say, "Hey, that's the guitarist who got shot in the ass." So now I'm writing a song about it. You ever heard of Buzzy Linhardt? That's who I'm staying with now. The band I'm into plays speed metal, and I'm a little too old for that. I'd rather get a blues thing going.

It grazed me, that's what they call it. It left a little canal, because of the leather pants it took a chunk out, about eight layers of skin. And still when I sit down it weirds me out because it still feels numb around that area. Actually, the nurse told me, "You'd have been better off if it had made total contact." Why? Then I'd have to go through surgery? Fuck that.

Those cops wanted to know everything. First of all, I hate cops. I really don't respect them at all. I know this girl that's going through the academy now, it's really fucking her up. I told this one detective, he said, "Well, if you want to sit down and rap about it," and I said, "Look, I hate cops. I hate any authority figure." He said, "Oh, are you an outlaw?" I said, "Yeah." Because I am. I'm known around here as an outlaw guitar player.

[Brooklyn] that's where I got this one back here [back of right shoulder]. You know where Peter Luger's is, the steak house? Right down the block. I was coming home one night, I was bagged out, tired, and one of these assholes said something to my lady. I had one of those big spiked belts on, so I whipped that off and called him out. Me and him were going at it and one of his boys come up behind me and shot me in the shoulder.

It spun the shit out of me. I walked from there to Fort Greene Hospital, right down Atlantic Avenue at three o'clock in the morning, blood pouring all over. That one went right through. They weren't sure what the hell [caliber] it was. I never went back to find out the ballistics or anything. In fact I never went back for the follow-up. They irrigated it and removed the fuckin' shrapnel and bandaged it up and said, "Come back to this clinic in a week." They gave me antibiotics and all that. I went to this bar and got drunk.

This here, this was a baseball bat to the forehead. I was about fifteen or sixteen. I thought I was Mr. Big Smoke Dealer. Someone owed me some money, and when I went to collect it he wasn't gonna pay and he got me with a bat.

This happened [left shin, small bullet scar], you know where Gaelic Park is in the Bronx? It's a little tiny park, it's not even really on the map. Back in the early '70s, the late '60s, they used to give concerts there, shows. I'd go up there with my angel dust and my weed, and these guys wanted to rip me off. Two of 'em got me down on the ground and said, "Okay fuckhead, think about that," *boom.*

I'm a white guy from the Lower East Side; who am I to go up to Little Puerto Rico and sell drugs? This guy that I knew from around here, he'd say, "Come on, man, let's go up to Gaelic Park" . . . at the time it was all rock bands, Starship, Hot Tuna, Bobby and the Midnights . . . it was right after the Fillmore closed. They used to rent out Gaelic Park.

Everybody tells me, "Yo, I should take an accident insurance policy out on you." Every week something's happening to me, you know? This here [long scar inside right elbow], this was over a bottle of Jack Daniel's. I was hanging out getting drunk, and this guy was being real rude to this girl. And in fact it was my bottle of Jack. I said, "Look, you can have the bottle or you can have the girl." Next thing I know there's a butterfly knife, *bing*. Oh, shit.

We went at it, we were on the street, this was on St. Marks between First and Avenue A. There used to be this little hole-in-the-wall bar called the International. We had that whole block, we went at it for about two hours. The Guardian Angels wouldn't step in, the Ninth Precinct wouldn't step in. This guy was bigger than I am, but I had the best of him until the knife. I was trying to get him in a headlock and I didn't even feel it. Next thing I know there's blood all over the place.

I was laid up with this arm for about two months. Stitched up and everything. Still, I don't have the coordination I should have.

Like here [left hand] I grabbed a knife out of someone's hand [the scar arcs across the ball of his thumb and palm close to the wrist]. I had to stop playing guitar for a couple of years because of that. When I wake up in the morning this [left forearm] is all numb. It cut everything, went right in. Two days later my hand blew up because they didn't clean it. What happened was, the guy apparently used a sharpening stone on his knife and the hospital didn't do a good cleaning job. They should have gone deeper. They should have cut into it like they were supposed to. It should have been X-rayed. If there's metal in there, the X-ray will show it. When I went back the doctor did this [light squeeze] and all this green and yellow shit oozed out. He said, "We did this?" I said, "Yeah, I wasn't here but forty-eight fucking hours ago." He said, "They didn't clean it." I said, "You mean they just numbed it up and stitched it and that's it?" He said, "Yeah."

St. Vincent's. Never go to St. Vincent's. I never felt so fucking humiliated. I had on a pair of six-hundred-dollar leather jeans; they cut 'em right off. They had me stripped in twenty seconds. And before they could even ask me questions I had all these fucking detectives there asking me everything.

"What were you doing down there? Would you look at a lineup? Can you describe the guy?" They say everything's confidential but that's a bunch of shit. Like the last time I got arrested they went through my keys and took one of these. They said, "Oh, you can't have that; that's a weapon." Whattaya mean that's a weapon, man, it's a nail file.

They said, "What's all the keys to?" I only own six grand in Marshall amps, so I keep them in different places, locked up. I got keys to my parents' house, to my girlfriend's house. "What's it to you? You wanna know when the last time I shit was?" They were going through everything.

I told them, I said, "I gotta go to the bathroom." They gave me a bedpan. Nobody's looking. All I had was my trenchcoat and I walked out of there with no clothes, just my trenchcoat and my boots. Went right down Greenwich, right up St. Marks. They gave me six stitches and some kind of cream, bacitracin, and some antibiotics. No painkillers. Because they looked up my drug history and said, "You can't have this." I said, "Admit me and give me Demerol."

It burned. You ever eat hot pepper? That's what it felt like. Everytime I'd move, oooh. It felt like heartburn sitting right on my hip. Everytime we go to rehearsal Ned goes, "How's your ass?" *Smack!*

Thirty-three years old and still streetfighting, outlaw guitarist Steve Fuller lives on New York's Lower East Side.

▪ ROGER KANE

I got shot in Vietnam, in 1968. March 16, 1968, to be exact. I lost my right kneecap.

I was in a helicopter at the time, we were coming out of a landing zone. As we banked over the treetops I was hit and the next thing I remember was waking up and my foot was rubbing against my elbow.

I was only about twenty feet off the ground when I got hit. We were dropping troops there. I was a gunner in the door of a Huey. They had staked the perimeter, brought in troops, dropped them off. We staircased our way in and out. Drop down, bank off, and I got hit off the treetops.

I don't know if you know the sound of a helicopter blade while you're in [the copter]. It's kind of loud, and you're wearing a helmet, but we could hear that we were taking fire. I didn't hear the one that hit me. All I could remember was feeling like my legs were on fire. I felt the hit like someone hit me in the knees with a baseball bat. Then I felt heat rush through my body like it lit me on fire. This rush of heat climbed up my body and the next thing I knew I was lying on the ground. I broke my wrist, too, but that was nothing compared to having your foot rubbing against your elbow. I was laying flat and my foot was over here, facing down. I thought I wasn't alone, to be honest.

I didn't know what to do at the time. I couldn't move, and being on the ground, where I wasn't used to being . . . I was only in Vietnam three months. What happened, I got a little nervous and decided to cover myself with leaves, whatever I could get my hands on, underbrush, things like that. I did, and I waited. I couldn't get up. I don't know how long it was, it could have been ten minutes, it felt like ten years. In fact it probably was ten years. I hear somebody saying, "*What the fuck,*" you know, guys talking, "*What the fuck are we doing out here?*" That's when I started saying, "Yo, over here please!" They called an evacuation to get me out of there. They asked where I was from. What could I say, "I came out of a helicopter." "*Well yeah, so did we.*" But I wasn't supposed to.

The doctors explained to me that the heat flowing through my body, the feeling, must have been shock. Sometimes shock puts you out, shuts your system down. The shock of getting hit in the knees, actually I got a little piece in the left knee, too . . . it could have come through the hull of the aircraft, too; it didn't have to be direct. I don't know how it actually happened. Front would have been tough; it had to come from underneath. We were twenty, thirty feet off the ground. It blew me right out the door. I wasn't hooked in, that was another problem. You should be.

When they picked me up it was a problem because my foot was rubbing against my elbow. They had to carry me. Actually what happened was the top of the kneecap shattered off and slid down inside the skin. The bottom part was disintegrated from getting hit, it got hit just on the edge. That could have stopped a lot of the damage. It went right through the knee joint. None of the arteries were damaged at all.

There was nerve damage, there's no feeling on the inside of my leg . . . I remember I was playing a little softball. I could feel some blood running down. You say, what the hell is that, you look down at your pants and you've got blood. You reach down and there's blood on your hands. Yet you didn't feel any injury.

I got hypersensitive feeling across my ankle. It sounds crazy, but I can't stand in the shower and let the water run down on my leg. It feels like something's happening to it.

I had drop foot for a while. I came back from it, thank God. I had it to the point where my foot would just lay there. That was because I had some nerve damage, and some of that came back. I got hit in '68, I'd say it got it back after a couple operations in 1970. After some physical therapy and stuff. It started coming back little by little. My foot's not as strong as the other one. I can't bend it all the way, and I can't straighten it out all the way. You can hold my foot down without any problem.

Of all the things I had, for the longest time, probably the most bothersome was tripping. It's a pain in the ass. There's nothing you can do; you're dragging your toe. There's no way you can, I mean, you can probably tie a string to the top of your toe or your leg, but that's not going to . . . that's the worst thing that happened to me, forever tripping, ripping my pants and shit.

I had a peroneal nerve operation, too. I don't know if that had anything to do with it. The peroneal nerve runs down the back of your leg and it crosses over at the knee and then goes down the front, and that's where the damage was. Where it crossed here [knee] is where I got damaged. It's a surface nerve. When they worked on that I started getting some of that [movement] back. And then they worked with me with the physical therapy. With the numbness, you don't have as much pain. So it wasn't like I had to take painkillers for the pain, because I had numbness. But boy, that [drop foot] was a pain in the ass. You can't run, you can't do anything to get in shape, you can't try anything when your foot's like that. If you're riding a bike you still have trouble getting any kind of control over the pedals. You try to push down with the balls of your feet, and you lock your feet in and you can't even pull up.

I always wore hightop sneakers. I still do. It makes your leg stiffen up. When you pick it up you're not really picking up your toes, but they pick up.

If you never suffered from drop foot, I tell you, nobody knows what you're going through. It's an amazing thing. I'm just glad that [movement] came back. Physical therapy, I think that brought it back some more. Heavy-duty aspirins; you ever go through that routine? Take a lot of aspirins so your knee doesn't swell up and exercise as hard as you can. Of course your knee doesn't swell up because there's no antibodies in there and then you get infections, and oh, what a pain in the ass then.

You got to remember, this was 1968, twenty-two years ago, and that's a long time. Luckily I was able to come back pretty far. I'm on the job nineteen years now and never really had a problem. I can still run pretty well. My leg gives out before my heart does, before my lungs do. My leg stiffens up because of all the arthritic spurs that I had. When something goes through your knee joint it tears all the cartilage out, tears out the collateral ligament and all that kind of shit, and goes out the back. Then you have to get all that fixed. I did that a few times. I'm not saying I could catch *anybody*, but I can do a lot of running. It really didn't slow me down a lot, thank God. It slowed me down for a couple years—it was about three years before I could get back and really do something—but I kept my weight down to about 170, and that's the toughest part now, getting under 190 . . . I'm lucky I have one good leg, that's what I always say.

I was eighteen and I was chomping at the bit. My mother had to put up with an awful lot. I was on crutches for a year. And in those days, in 1968, you didn't rebuild knees. This was a new thing to rebuild a knee. Not that I was a new thing, it was being done. But you didn't do it; they straightened your leg out, made it straight. I refused to make it straight. So for a long time I had a hard time walking on it, like I say, falling down all the time. Brace after brace, I must have twelve braces at home. They never really worked.

I was a Paterson [New Jersey] cop for ten years before I came here. The first thing we did was walk a beat. Walk a beat, rode in a patrol car, tactical patrol units, things like that. And like I said, I tried staying up on the sports I could do, little bit of basketball, some softball. It would hurt, and I had to have an operation here and there to fix what I did wrong.

I never was going to let it get me down. From the day it happened, from when they told me, *"You're going to have a hard time walking, kid, much less running,"* you can't make me believe that. If I fell down once I fell down a thousand times, but I got up a thousand and one times. That's exactly how I felt: I wasn't going to stay down, it wasn't going to keep me down. I see guys now, athletes having knee operations and their careers are gone . . . bullshit. I had nine knee operations. If I had the time I could get in shape and run again. It's going to hurt, it's going to swell up and cause me problems, but it's mine. I've got it, I'm going to use it. They say, "Take it easy, it'll last forever." I don't care if it lasts forever. You got to enjoy what you got. I can run, I can stand up. So I lost a little feeling here and there, so it's a little bothersome. But other than that, it's been a hell of a road. It's something to remember.

Roger Kane is a detective sergeant with the Bergen County, New Jersey, Prosecutor's Office, Department of Special Investigations. He has a plastic kneecap.

■ Big Daddy

It was December 21st, a cold day. I worked for Walker Oil
delivering fuel oil. I was a truck driver. Eight o'clock at night
I get a call to go to Rose Avenue in Jersey City, near Martin
Luther King Drive. It has the highest crime rate in Hudson
County. Nothing there but stone-cold junkies, and they're
everywhere. The burner was out of oil, so I was gonna deliver what I had left in the truck and go home.

I get down there, set everything up, I stick the tank, everything's fine, everything's normal. I'm putting the oil in the
ground, an hour goes by, another hour goes by, and now it's
like ten thirty. I saw some guy passing the truck and it didn't
look right, didn't feel right. He was walking on the street. So
I took the cash box and stashed it underneath some rags on
the side of the truck and then I walked around the other
side. I was gonna hang out a little bit.

I went inside for a second because there was a burner
man checking out the burner. Then I came back out and
said, "Let me check the truck, it's gotta be just about empty
now." There was a compartment in the back of the truck
where the hose reel was, and all that other shit. I stuck my
head in there. I was running a White Diesel, very noisy. Oil
trucks are very noisy when they're empty. The valve hadn't
shut off, there was a defect in it. It just didn't operate prop-
erly, it malfunctioned. The meter kept turning as if there
was fuel in there but it was just pumping air.

I felt somebody push me, and I thought the burner man wanted to tell me something. I turned around and these guys shot me though the elbow and tried to rob me. They got seventy-one cents and an empty wallet, that's what they got. Two black guys, I believe they were junkies. I didn't go after them.

It was a fucked-up feeling, because if I'd have grabbed a pipe I'd have bashed 'em both in the brains. They were no threat to anybody without that gun. Maybe at most they were 130 pounds, both of them. The one guy—I'm holding my elbow and I started screaming obscenities at the guy, calling him a dirty motherfucker, I called him everything under the sun, "You cocksucking nigger I'll kill you." He backed up. He took six steps back which put him about eight feet from me, so I couldn't get near him. So I said, "What do you want, man?"

"Gimme money."

"I don't have no fucking money. You came on the wrong day. I get paid tomorrow."

"Gimme what you got."

So I gave him the change. Seventy-one cents. Big deal. That's what he got for the whole thing, a cup of coffee. The bullet probably cost him more. So then he went across the street and robbed the service man, too. Then I walked inside holding my arm and a lady called the cops and I was off to the Jersey City Medical Center.

It was a small-caliber bullet, a .22, probably a .22 with a long barrel. I remember the barrel, about that long [six inches]. We had a lawsuit in. I got a scar on my elbow, I had bone fragments, bullet fragments. It aches a little bit now.

The biggest thing was that it set a pattern. A couple years later I was involved in a fight in a bar that turned into total violence. Two boys almost died because of a knife. One doctor said this was "all based off of you being attacked. Somewhere in your mind you were not going to be a victim anymore. So you weren't. When these two guys approached, you just let it all out." For which I did time in jail, and I'm doing time on parole. . . .

See, I'm a man that's been around outlaw bike clubs for twenty years. I live in a world of constant confusion. That's what bike clubs are about, that's what outlaws are about, that's what bikers are about. They all live on a fine-honed edge. I've ridden with the toughest, I've ridden with the not-so-tough. I've hung out with the baddest. I was considered to be one of the three most dangerous men in Jersey at this point because of the last crime, the last thing I got involved in.

When you run on that edge, man, and somebody takes you down and there's no way physically that he could do it, and he's a dirtbag to boot, you get messed up in your head. I did time in 'Nam, I did the whole nine yards. You get messed up in your head because you can't deal with it. You know what you're capable of, and you know they're *not* capable of doing that because of who you are. I guess it burns an impression into your head that some jerk somewhere with a peashooter just took you out. Or tried to take you out. And it hurts. It stays in your brain.

I've played Santa Claus for little kids, and there's never been a day come by in my life that I wouldn't be willing to help somebody if they needed it. I'll come down, give you a ride, help you out. If you need help I'll be there. That's the way I am. That's what I base my life off of. And for a long time after I was shot you couldn't sneak up on me; I'd rip your head off.

I swore to myself I'd never be taken down again. I don't care who it is. In order to take me down you gotta kill me. To take me out like that, I mean, if I could have gotten something off the truck that was long enough I would have bashed 'em both in the head, taken the gun, and shot 'em both dead where they were; 'cause you don't take me out like that. I don't go that way.

I'm not crazy, I'm just the way I've always been. I've ridden with heavy people and that's the way our life-style is. It's the one-percent life-style and you ain't taking me out. Nobody's taking me out. I've been in a lot of heavy skirmishes, I've been in a lot of different situations. If it's coming down I'm dealing it.

A little junkie weasel like that, if you punch him in the face you get AIDS. You end up with this slimeball's blood all over your body and your things fall off in five years. I figure somewhere down the road the guy will score a hot bag of dope or something, and his buddy'll want it, and his buddy'll borrow his gun and blow his brains out. Happens every day. And I don't have to chase him down. And if he feels impressed by what he did then he's just stupid.

I'm not concerned. I'm not afraid of anything; guns, bullets, knives, don't bother me. Take your best shot, because when it's over I'm taking mine. Unless I get to it first.

Oh, by the way, I saved the cash box. The boss got it, then he never called me again. That's because he's a lowlife citizen squid bastard rich fuck . . . and a friend of mine.

It was stupid. It was something I never expected in ninety-five years. He just fractured the elbow bone. The caliber was small enough that . . . they said if it was a large caliber it would have taken the elbow out. I lost a tremendous amount of blood. I was under guard at the hospital and while under guard one of the cops came to me and said, "We know who you are, we know what you're about. We don't want any trouble."

"Don't want any trouble? In case you hadn't noticed I'm laying here with the bullet hole. There's nobody next to me. What trouble are you talking about?"

"Well, we have a file."

"Good for you." It was Jersey City, where the old Nomads were from. I was an old Nomad a long time. "We have a file, we know all you guys. We don't want any trouble."

I told the cop, I said, "You know what the problem is, man? The trouble is on your streets and you can't cure it. You can't solve your own problems. I'm not gonna offer you no trouble. I want to go home. I'm in a sleazebag hospital, eating shit that I wouldn't feed to my dog, and I want to go home."

They didn't want to hear that, because I rode with a bike club and I was a bad guy. "I'm the guy laying here with the hole in my arm, man. Go out and find the guys that shot me. Get out." Then, when I'm in the emergency room they gave me a black detective to cover my ass. I said, "Can you please get out of my face? I've seen enough black guys for one night, and I don't trust you. Get away from me." The next morning I apologized to the guy because he did not leave my side. He sat there like he was ordered to do. Because they thought it was a hit. They thought it was a contract. "You guys are out of your brains, man. You're really nuts." They play "One Adam Twelve" no matter what happens. It's amazing. That's why they can't catch criminals, because they're too stupid looking for everything else that doesn't matter.

In fact the night I got in the fight with those guys, [they said] "suspected drug deal." What drug deal? I don't do drugs. What are they talking about? Maybe those guys were dealing drugs, maybe that was their business. I don't know, I've never seen these bums before in my life. . . .

I grew up in Hackensack, and the guys I went to school with, a lot of 'em became cops. I'm still good friends with a lot of 'em, and I respect 'em because they've made a decision to do a tough job. It's a very tough job. You've got guys out there with shit the armies don't have. And they're not playing. The whole game is different, it's not 1929 when you had one shoot-out a week. Now they're killing people left and right. The problem is sometimes they get overzealous and sometimes they underreact. It just depends on what kind of mood they're in.

For instance, this fight I got into. I was sentenced to seven years. I got out on parole. But the two guys that started the fight didn't get anything. They didn't even see the judge. Now, I admitted that I was wrong, but I didn't provoke it, all I did was end it. The outcome was disastrous, I can tell you that right now. It was not something that I ever pictured my-self doing in a situation like that.

Two beer-muscle drunk boys, 'cause that's what they come out to be. They never even showed up in court. Where does the law change? How come we don't have a standard set of rules for everybody? If you have a lot of money, you can get off on a charge like that.

It was me against two guys. I won. How's that. I was the winner—understand? There was a lot of confusion. Both of them went to the hospital, one guy had to have surgery, 'cause they both got stabbed. It's nothing I'm proud of, be-cause they weren't even adversaries. They weren't people I even knew. They were strangers with too many beer muscles trying to impress a go-go girl. That's what it come down to. The one that egged 'em on, she's the worst of all because that's all she's good for, trouble. And they didn't know it. And at the time I was too drunk to realize it. Plus the fact that I had a real bad week, so the whole thing was one big disaster. But it cost me time off my life, which you can't get back, and all because it's just beer-muscle time. People get beer muscles, and they shouldn't be there. But the law doesn't handle it equally. According to the law you're sup-posed to be able to face your accusers. The prosecutor takes the place of the two guys I had the fight with? How come the law varies just because you don't have any money?

The judge said, "Mister, I would appeal this." I said, "Your honor, you got ten thousand dollars you want to lend me? I'll do it." He was being fair with me. He was a streetwise judge; he's now dead, but he was an honest judge.

It was a bizarre situation, but it all stems from being shot. The cops were around the corner having coffee in the local coffee shop. They know that this is a crime area . . . they passed me twice. You know that there's a white man in a heavy-crime area, in a black ghetto where they constantly do this shit. Now, the white and black thing doesn't mean any-thing, but that's how you describe it. What were they doing in the coffee shop? Why don't you do your job and be where it could happen, or come by and say, "How much longer are you gonna be here," or "I'll leave one guy by you because of . . ." If you can't control the crime in your town, I'm sorry. Everyone knows that crime is at an outrageous rate.

Big Daddy resides in northern New Jersey, as he has all his life.

■ Dean R. Kahler

I was shot at Kent State University in 1970 on May the fourth, approximately 12:25 or 12:30, somewhere in that general vicinity. The situation surrounding the shooting was that Thursday, April 30, Richard Nixon had made an announcement that he would invade Cambodia. Actually it was Thursday night. And on Friday, May the first, there were protests all across the country against the invasion of Cambodia.

The shootings at Kent happened on a Monday after the announcement on Thursday night. It was after a long weekend of related and unrelated violence that happened in the community of Kent and around the Kent State University campus. Friday night there were some people who started a fire in some trash cans downtown and rolled them out into the middle of the street. That attracted a lot of people out of the bars. The people who were in charge of law enforcement and the mayor at that point in time thought it was a wise idea to post a curfew and close the town down and chase these thousands of people who were in bars and hadn't come out in other parts of the city out into the street and herd them like cattle down towards the campus.

Kent State, like some college campuses around the country, is a commuter campus, being surrounded by Akron, Canton, Cleveland, and Youngstown. Most people commuted to Kent, most didn't live on campus. So being herded down Main Street toward the campus was not most people's idea of where they wanted to go. They wanted to go back to their automobiles wherever they were parked.

So that caused people, I think, to break some windows and cause some damage to storefronts near the campus. Part of the reason that all this was happening was that in the weeks before the shooting happened, and before April 30-May 1st, Richard Nixon and Spiro Agnew had been going around the country calling us bums, all kinds of nasty names, trying to paint a them-against-us picture.

During the '68 campaign he promised the American public that he had a way to end the war. It was a secret, though, he wasn't going to tell anybody. This is now a year and a half into his first term of office, no real changes have been happening in Vietnam. It looks as though, to us, that the war in Vietnam was going to be expanded—that more of my friends were going to be going to Vietnam, that more of my friends were coming home from Vietnam with injuries, in boxes, coming home acting crazy, which we now know is delayed stress syndrome. So there was this big situation where Richard Nixon was very paranoid and very upset that young people, and sometimes people who could vote—back then you had to be twenty-one to vote—were disputing his foreign policy in Southeast Asia. He didn't like that a bit. So he painted this picture that there were people out there who were against the war and against America. And if you were against America there was something wrong with you. He was pitting two segments of society against each other, the rednecks and the hardhats, to use an example, against the hippies, basically.

This was sort of, I think, what led to the tension that caused the mayor of Kent to, first of all, close the town down on Friday and call a curfew and create the hysteria that he did. And also led to him calling out the Ohio National Guard the next day, on Saturday. Richard Nixon, basically, had found himself a willing partner.

Something else that was part of the whole picture here that caused tension to be so tough between the students and nonstudents: the governor of the state of Ohio was running for the U.S. Senate in a very closely contested primary battle over his nomination. Being an old-line politician, he felt that people should listen to what the governor says and do what the governor tells you to do. He came to the campus on Sunday, after some people—I'm not going to say students—burned down the ROTC building, to survey the damage and to get tough. They were going to keep this campus open, keep the National Guard here. They were going to take over, which is contrary to standard operating procedure. They were going to run the campus and they were going to keep it open.

The reason I said that "some people" burned down the ROTC building, if you read the FBI report, most of the other reports that were done after the shooting at Kent State University agree that the ROTC building was burned down by suspicious causes, and that students in no way attempted the fire or [to] burn down the ROTC building. Makes you wonder who was attempting to do it when the authorities were standing around with their hands in their pockets watching them do it.

So anyway, Governor Rhodes was there on Sunday. He came there and made a very inflammatory speech, saying that they were taking over, picking up the words of Richard Nixon, calling us bums, the worst element we harbor in our society. It sort of set the stage for the animosity and hatred between the students and the Guard after they had been there for a day or so.

So Monday, the next day, the first day of class after the long weekend of violence, vandalism, and arson of some sort, the National Guard troops weren't supposed to let crowds gather of more than four people. By noontime there were several thousand people who had gathered on the commons. The commons area is an area in the center of the campus which has the student center on one side and a very large classroom building on the other side, and other classroom buildings just across the street from the student center. Plus about half a dozen dormitories, all within eyesight of the commons area.

Put that into consideration with the fact that Kent is primarily a commuter campus. At that time they had about 21,000 students going to school there. So you put all these factors together, and you put them into a situation where students were gathering for a rally that was announced on Friday, on May the first, to protest the invasion of Cambodia. Add several thousand people who had nowhere to go, to the dormitories, to the classrooms, or to the student center where they were going to go get a meal. Or, it being the first nice, warm day we'd had that spring—Kent's in a snow belt, it snows a lot—people were outside anyway.

So they were all gathered in one area, they were all there, and the National Guard were on one end and the students were on the other end. They came out and read the riot act and chased people around with tear gas. And they didn't do a good job of dispersing the crowd from where they were. So instead of stopping and seeing where the students ended up, they reread the riot act and chased the students around, dispersing the crowd. After it was broken up into smaller pockets, they kept on going toward the students. They went up over the hill, down the other side of the hill, into a practice football field that was surrounded on three sides by a fence. The students basically formed a fourth fence on the other side.

At that point in time they loaded their weapons [and] pointed them at a group of students that were in another direction, say 45 degrees away from where the other students—maybe 90 degrees—away from where they were forming the fourth fence.

They huddled back together finally, and marched back up the hill parting the sea of students on their way to the top of the hill, where they had just come from—part of their path from where they had originally started from. They started in a low area, went up over the hill, down the other side of the hill, down into the practice football field. Then they marched back up to the top of the hill where they had just come from. When they reached the top of the hill, they turned and fired.

My own personal recollection of all of this was that when they were marching up the hill, I said to myself, "They're just going to go to the top of the hill and use tear gas all afternoon and send out little groups to break up the little pockets of students that were gathered here, there, and everywhere."

At the time when they reached the top of the hill and turned and fired, I said to myself, "Oh my God, they're shooting at me." I could hear the bullets ricocheting off the blacktop near where I was standing, and I could hear the M1 rifle rounds going into the ground near where I was standing as well. There was no place to cover, to hide for cover. I remember jumping on the ground and covering my head and praying that I wouldn't get hit. Then all of a sudden, toward the end of the volley, which lasted about thirty seconds, I got shot.

I remember it hitting me and my nerves, my legs getting real tight and relaxing. It's like a very severe bee sting. It lasted only for a split second. I didn't bleed externally, I bled internally primarily.

The shooting continued for a split second or so and then stopped. There was an eerie silence, and then severe chaos. There was a little chaos going on during the shooting but nothing like what happened afterward. Thirty people were wounded and four of those people were dying on the ground right in front of people. Those of us who couldn't get up were laying on the ground and those who could get up were wandering around with wounds on their hands, arms, legs, wherever they were shot.

I couldn't get up; I was wounded with a spinal cord injury. I remember laying on the ground after I got shot and saying to myself, "Relax, take it easy, don't freak out." I hadn't passed out, I was still wide awake during the whole process. Someone came to me and asked me who I was, and asked me if I wanted them to roll me over. I said, "No, I don't want you to touch me, I have a back injury." I was sort of directing the people around me. I knew quite a bit about first aid and I wasn't going to let anybody touch me who didn't know what they were doing. And then I gave them my parents' telephone number, where they were working at, I had it in memory, and they went and called them. [My parents] didn't have to find out about the shooting from the television. I had somebody else tell them. They were called directly within five minutes of my being shot.

I remember laying there and seeing the horrified look on these students who were standing around me looking down at me, the amazing look of disbelief in their eyes. That's something I still remember to this day, what people looked like who were looking at me laying on the ground. Horrified. These people who were there had to witness the whole process.

That's basically the situation surrounding my shooting. I spent three weeks in intensive care and went into the rehab center until October 25, 1970. I was released and I've basically been out since.

I'm a quick healer and I'm a very strong person to begin with. I was an athlete before I got hurt. I have a strong body, a strong heart, and a strong will. Also I'm an old farm boy from northeastern Ohio. You get up in the morning, you put your pants on, and you go to work. You work until dark, you relax a little bit, go to sleep, and you get up and do it again. You had a little fun once in a while, whenever you get a chance to. I had a pretty strong will to live and to get rehabbed and out of the hospital. I didn't like being in the hospital. I'm a quick learner, too. That comes from doing physical-type things.

It was definitely a public-type situation. I had interviews with the FBI, the Justice Department, the President's Commission on Student Unrest, news media. . . . I remember when I was wheeled into the rehab hospital after I'd left the general hospital. I was being wheeled in and the whole hallway got quiet. People stuck their heads out the doors from the rooms to see this wild-eyed crazy guy from Kent who was coming in. Little did they know I had horn-rimmed glasses and short hair, bright red hair. I didn't look all too radical—

actually pretty conservative . . . not the wild-eyed crazy hip-
pie they were expecting.

When I got to the hospital I remember hearing a nurse or
a doctor or somebody saying, "Get blood types on all these
people." I remember reaching in my wallet and pulling out
my driver's license, my student ID, my blood donor's card,
my insurance card, and Social Security card. I figured those
were the kinds of things that hospitals need. And they were
quite pleased that I had my blood donor's card, it saved
them a lot of time. I was still awake, I stayed awake through
this whole process. When I was laying there waiting to go
into the operating room someone showed up that I knew, a
minister friend of mine who had been called by my mother
and father. He lived near there and he came to visit me and
we had a nice long chat, prayed together, and I went into
the operating room. I had a set of beads from a girlfriend,
and I was starting to get delirious at this point in time, and I
remember saying, *"Get these beads off of me,"* and they
wouldn't take them off so I just ripped them off and I remember hearing all these little beads going all over the
floor.

[Kahler was in a coma for four days after surgery.] My experience of waking up, coming out of the coma I was in
were—I don't know if they were bizarre or not, but they
were bizarre to me. I remember waking up and being very
sore, having a lot of pain, and hearing voices before I could
even see. I heard people around me. Then I came into consciousness and of course I was in intensive care.

I was surprised I didn't bleed a whole lot. I'm told that an
M1 rifle is very powerful. A .30-caliber rifle is what it is. It
usually makes a very small incision when it goes in and a
very large hole when it comes out. Mine made a very large
hole going in, about the size of my thumbnail, and no hole
going out because it didn't go out. It stayed in me. They theorized that an M1 will go through things if they're not very
substantial, and when it does that it flattens the bullet out
just a little bit bigger. If it hits something after it's slowed

down, it'll make a big hole. So they theorized it went through something before it hit me. Whether it was burrowing under the ground, which they can do, just under the sod, or through a tree, or it went through something else. . . .

In my case they couldn't figure out why I lived. There was damage to my lungs, damage to my diaphragm, and I bled internally pretty extensively. I was full of blood when they opened me up. I don't remember how many pints of blood I lost, but I lost a tremendous amount of blood. Internally I lost a lot of blood. And they sewed me up with silk, as opposed to gut, because they were in such a hurry to sew me back up and get me on life-support systems and keep me alive. And I was out of it like I say until early Thursday morning, three or four in the morning.

So a year later, all the stitches that they sewed me up with on the inside started coming out. Big pockets of pus, abscesses, you know? I went to the doctor a couple of times and figured out, "Hey, I can do that myself, you know?" I can just cut this big abscess, drain it out with a sterile cloth, reach in there with a sterile probe, and cut the [stitch] off and pull it out. So I did. I've got a whole jar of stitches that I pulled out myself.

My bullet's still in me and it shows up on X-rays. I can always tell when a doctor is looking at an X-ray in the hospital on me—when I go in for a checkup—when the doctor who is reading the X-rays hasn't read the chart. The question always comes back to me when I'm laying on the table there, on the X-ray table: what the hell have I got on, or is there something in me? I have to explain to the X-ray technician, "Yes, there is a bullet inside of me."

Still in a wheelchair, Dean R. Kahler is serving his second term as a county commissioner in Athens County, Ohio. He took time out from fixing his yard tractor to talk.

■ DUM DUM

In the early summer, after I'd worked a couple of dozen jobs in the five months since my discharge from the Marine Corps, I realized I had a problem: I couldn't relate to anyone who wasn't a 'Nam vet. They couldn't understand anything I had to say and I didn't give a damn about things other people thought were important. Basically, it was mind over matter: I didn't mind and they didn't matter.

I decided to resume my habit of annual pilgrimages from Florida—where I lived—up the eastern seaboard to . . . anywhere north. I'd made it as far as Toronto, Canada, once. The important part was the going, not the destination. I always traveled back roads, partying and making friends everywhere I went. It was a pleasant educational way to spend a couple months.

Since I had never actually seen most of the beach on the Atlantic Coast and my alma mater, so to speak—Parris Island—was along the route, I pointed my Sportster north and let the clutch out. I was born in California and raised in central Florida, so I wasn't ready for the big surprise: most of the beachfront property through Georgia and South Carolina are either swamps or sloughs that smell like a sewage treatment plant, or are owned by rich snobs who hire rent-a-cops to chase away tourists.

I was too angry to think straight when the Marine M.P.s refused to allow me on the base at Parris Island, or I might have realized things had changed—America had changed—and abandoned the entire quest.

The cops in Charleston were nice enough to let me sit under the eave of a closed fast-food restaurant to get out of the rain and nap for two hours before politely telling me to get the hell out of Dodge. They were quite nice about it, really.

By the time I reached Myrtle Beach, I closely examined several brands of beer bottles as they flew past my head, and been taunted by a carload of kids—my own age—with a twelve-gauge pump shotgun. Real friendly folks. Far too many people, it seems, were adversely motivated by that great, classic flick, *Easy Rider.*

I stayed for a week of badly needed R&R just outside Myrtle Beach in the old Fort Caroline that some movie company had completely restored. A bunch of hippies had leased it. It was great, there was a beautiful little redhead . . . well, anyway it was outstanding until the good citizens of the area (Myrtle Beach is a tourist town) figured out how to break the hippies' lease and sent the state police and the National Guard in to evict everyone. At bayonet-point. More friendly folks. I was really starting to become disillusioned with this new America I was discovering!

The coast and I parted company as I entered North Carolina and turned left to bisect the state and head for the Smokies. I partied the width of the state without a sour note. I was impressed and encouraged by the hospitality extended by the people throughout the state. This was more like the America I'd grown up in, where folks were carefree, kind, and generally neighborly. One interesting aspect of this adventure—in retrospect—was that it only rained on me in places where the locals were hostile or afraid of me. I've never believed in omens, evil or otherwise, or I might have become a bit paranoid on that trip.

At the time, I dismissed my uneasiness to being in the Great Smoky Mountains National Park. Don't get me wrong, that part of the country is some of the most beautiful and scenic real estate in the world, and I've seen plenty of turf. It was because of an experience I'd had a few years earlier in the same area: I'd discovered, the hard way, why people don't sleep on picnic tables in bear country. The bruins like to stroll across the tabletops looking for groceries. I'd wound up nose-to-nose with a medium-sized black bear while it was standing on my chest. It's probably just as well that its weight forced all the air out of my lungs. I couldn't frighten the critter by doing a lot of unnecessary screaming. It went away after licking my face a couple of times, obviously having decided I was inedible. Needless to say, I'm not real fond of bears that aren't surrounded by a nice zoo.

I'd long since gotten used to the rain and being wet. I have never, however, been able to be comfortable in a sodden environment without adequate shelter; being curled up under a poncho just doesn't get it after a day or two. I wasn't a marine anymore and little unpleasantries like having water flow around my ass tended to bother me. I was a tad grouchy from sleep deprivation when I rolled into Gatlinburg.

Someday, before I die, I want to return to Gatlinburg and window-shop. I know that sounds weird, but hey, I'm a freak for swap meets, surplus stores, and good tourist traps. That town has the biggest, most interesting collection of tourist-oriented junk shops I've ever almost seen. The first time through, my dad was driving and he won't even slow down in a tourist town unless they set up roadblocks. This time I was driving, but representatives of the local law enforcement agency were busy escorting me firmly but gently through their lovely little town. Window-shopping from a moving motorcycle, over everyone's head, is no fun at all. Very hospitable.

As the sun began to set and the rain showed no sign of letting up, I started to entertain the notion of spending some of my very limited resources to get a motel room. While I was at it, I figured to take advantage of the lower drinking age and have a few legal brews.

This was along a stretch of two-lane that seemed to curve endlessly, from out of the dark, past the bike and into the darkness ahead, beside a happy little river named—I think—

the French Broad. There's no darkness except in a mine shaft quite like what you'll find on an overcast night in the middle of nowhere. Someplace between Gatlinburg and Knoxville I rounded a curve and suddenly came upon a motel and general store/tavern. It was almost like one of those "Twilight Zone" trips. I was so surprised I almost laid the bike down trying to stop on the slippery pavement.

So far on the trip I'd stayed in only one motel because the manager of most inns were prone to act like I had anthrax or some other weird disease. I camped out a lot or crashed at sociable people's pads. I turned the Sportster around and parked, splitting the distance between the public house and the motel next door.

After twenty minutes of proving I was me, in triplicate, and receiving a lecture on how it wasn't moral for a teenager to be renting a motel room—whereupon I had to prove my "worldliness" by convincing this Bible-thumping hayseed I was a veteran (I still had fresh scars)—I got a key and moseyed over to the pub.

I was halfway through the first swallow of swill that was on tap when some huge anthropoid at the far end of the bar hollered, "Hey, shitbag, we don' like your kind aroun' here!" I could barely understand him, but I was reasonably sure he was addressing me since everyone else—all three of them—had moved when I walked up. I gave myself the quick little social test my granny had taught me, checking if my armpits or breath smelled. Nope. I was soggy but I didn't smell too bad. I decided to ignore the humongous redneck for as long as possible. He had one of those helmets with a little head-light—a miner's hat—with about three hundred pounds of muscle and callus under it.

I had two of my favorite infighting toys on me, but I wasn't crazy about the odds, being in hostile territory, or the thought of abandoning a warm, dry bed I'd already paid for. One toy, the most obvious, was my K-Bar marine survival knife. The other, with the strap intertwined in my fingers, was my trusty helmet. I said a silent prayer to St. Christopher just to be extra safe. Maybe this big fool would pass out and fracture several bones—his own—when he contacted the floor.

I've always found it fascinating the way time seems to warp into slow motion and my thoughts flow so quickly and smoothly in moments of extreme danger. It's a condition I refer to as "battle mode." I did all sorts of wishful thinking in the forty-five seconds it took the moron to figure out I hadn't answered him yet.

"I'll bet you're one a those draft dodgers," he yelled. "Ya need a haircut, too!" I wasn't partial to having idiots infer that I'm cowardly. And my personal grooming was none of his business. My hair was just starting to get long enough so I could blend in at parties. I was fond of my hair. I stopped hoping he'd fall down and shifted my weight for combat.

My mouth overrode my brain as I quietly said, "I was in Hue, asshole. I don't recall seein' you there." I still don't know where he got the butcher knife from, but it was pretty obvious what he had in mind: he was going to scalp me. Or worse. The giant advanced, growling.

As he grabbed for my head, his halitosis heavy in the air, I kicked him firmly under the left kneecap, spun away, and swung my helmet, striking him on the temple. The redneck dropped like a stone, conscious and cussing. Knowing that discretion is often the better part of valor—especially in hostile territory—I beat feet out the door.

The kick-start pedal was on the downstroke when the gorilla swarmed through the door. I heard an anemic little pop as the engine roared into life, and felt a sharp jab on the front of my spine. I'd never felt a pain like that before. It reminded me of the focused shock of a chisel striking a concrete block, or like being hit with a steel bar.

It took me a few microseconds to realize I'd been shot, because I didn't feel anything unusual after the impact of the bullet. The redneck seemed surprised that I hadn't fallen down, or that the pistol he was holding had actually fired—I couldn't tell which. There was no way I was going to make it out of range before he fired again, so I hit the kill switch, threw myself off the far side of the Sportster, and pulled my last-resort toy from inside the seat. It was a fully automatic M1 carbine cut down to the size of a machine pistol. I was a sharpshooter in the Marine Corps, so I returned fire with a vengeance—fifteen shots in less than a second.

The redneck squawked once and collapsed in a heap. I could hear him wheezing, so I knew he was alive, and that was confirmed by my visual of the impact area; I'd nailed him three or more times in the chest. I started to get up, to restart my bike, when my gut and lumbar vertebra decided to remind me that I'd been shot. Suddenly sitting in the gravel sounded pretty good.

The barrel of the carbine was still smoking when the first sheriff's deputy showed up. He must have been close by. I tossed the useless carbine—I only had one clip of ammo—to the ground so deputy dog wouldn't blast me with the large-caliber hog leg he was pointing at my skull. He went to check on the gorilla.

His eyes went round and he exclaimed, "Aw, shit! It's ___ Bob!" I never did catch that name. The cop sprinted back to his patrol car—all of thirty feet—and started babbling into the Motorola. Apparently ol' Bob Bob was some VIP's brother. Far out. I was stuck in rural Tennessee with a bullet in my gut and about to be overwhelmed by nepotism.

I was still sitting on the gravel, getting more and more light-headed, when another cop, an older one, showed up with an ambulance. They carefully loaded the Neanderthal onto the gurney and into the meat wagon. Then they came back for me. The younger one grabbed my leathers, hauled me to my feet, and punched me in the teeth. I was cooperative—I fell back down. He kicked me in the ribs before I started yelling that I'd been shot, too. That got their attention. I guess it hadn't occurred to them to wonder why I'd just been sitting in the dirt beside a perfectly good Harley.

They dragged me over and sat me down in a jump seat in the back of the ambulance beside Joe Bob. He coughed, wheezed, and cussed at me. The attendant had removed his shirt and I started counting entry holes on him. I saw seven before the car's motion caused me to shift position. This guy was a tough SOB. I was impressed. I was also in pain; my guts felt like someone had started a barbecue behind and under my stomach.

At the hospital Billy Bob and I parted company after the X-rays were taken. The doc gave me a shot for the pain but said he wanted me awake to help him. I started to say something about the two large-breasted nurses standing there when he poked a finger into my abdomen. I lost all enthusiasm for witty repartee in a hurry. He enlarged the entry wound and probed around in my spinal column until he removed a .22-caliber slug.

The nurses got involved as he started pouring clear fluids into my abdomen while one nurse used a vacuum hose to suck it back out. He made several sutures while mumbling about peritonitis and damned sheriffs. The other nurse used gauze pads to scoop up tiny bits of foreign matter.

I had all kinds of anxiety by the time he's laid in a dozen stitches to close the wound. All I got out of him was that I was being released to the sheriff and I should watch for signs of infection. Very encouraging news.

After proving for the nine-hundredth time that I was, indeed, a 'Nam vet, the sheriff told me to sign a waiver and hit the road. Whatever VIP ol' Jim Bob was related to didn't want to press charges since the fool had long priors for assault, and even though I looked pretty scroungy and had an illegal weapon I was a decorated war hero. It wouldn't look good. God bless the Marine Corps! I signed the waiver so I couldn't sue anyone and split. The sheriff kept the carbine, of course.

I've got the recuperative powers of a flat worm, but I was still having minor problems a year later when I got married. Every time I'd try to hold in gas the pressure on my colon would cause me considerable pain until I flatulated soundly. Later, after my wife and I started having problems—she kept getting confused about who she was supposed to be screwing—I developed "spastic colitis." That's an inflammation of the colon. I had attacks of colitis until I discovered it's aggravated by nervous stress and followed the marriage counselor's advice: "Gracefully assist her in leaving." No problem. I signed over the car, gave her $50, and waved a lot.

I've felt pretty good ever since, although I do still have occasional muscle spasms in my lower back because of the damage from that tiny bullet.

The author of this piece, Dum Dum, is serving a life term in a Nevada prison.

■ Pat Delehanty

I would never want it to happen again, believe me. We went on a camping trip right out of high school, 1974. I went with one friend, Tom. We were doing a lot of drinking and partying, as usual. We were in Vermont, on a friend's property. He owned a hundred acres and we were camping for about a week, just in a tent, out in the woods.

[Tom] was using one of this guy's guns; he had a converted .45, I had a pistol, and we were doing a lot of target shooting on and off. Unfortunately, and it was my fault, we were doing a lot of fooling around with guns, a lot of stupid things.

That day I was sitting about four foot ahead of him, we were drinking and stuff, and as a matter of fact it was near dinnertime. I heard a shot go off and I thought, honestly, that he threw something at my knee and shot in the air. I felt something in my leg, it didn't hurt a lot, and he said, "My God, did I shoot you?" And I turned around and said, "Yeah, sure, asshole, you shot me." But I saw his face and a chill just came over me to think that I was shot.

It didn't hurt at all until that instant. It felt like a stone hit me. A very small pain. But then again, we had had plenty of Budweisers and pain wasn't really a thing then. We were about three-quarters of a mile from the guy's house, we didn't have a car, we had been dropped off up there, and the worst part was the ride to the hospital.

I just looked down and there was a hole in my pants. It

was an actual army .45 but they have a conversion kit that makes it a .22. *Fortunately* it was in the holster when it went off. Actually it went through a metal rivet. Luckily. Which is the reason why it didn't do a lot of damage. It was in his holster and he was obviously playing with it—he said he wasn't, he said it went off, but I know enough about guns, I mean, that has a grip safety. . . .

So anyway it hit me in the knee, and fortunately it had gone through the holster and stuff, and when I looked there was nothing, no blood. It didn't bleed at all, as a matter of fact, one drop. It sealed itself up. The bullet didn't come out of my leg, it went in. And as I said I can't really describe the pain because I was anesthetized when it happened.

It sobered me up, naturally, because you're half a mile in the woods and you're saying to yourself, "I'm shot." And that was scarier than the pain, because there really wasn't any pain.

We went to the hospital, which up there is an experience in itself. There were no doctors. I laid on the table for half an hour because the doctor was out fishing. (laughs) When the doctor did come, he starts explaining to me what happened, which I told him, "I know what happened, there's a bullet in here, here it is." I could feel the lump under my knee, I knew where it was. It didn't really swell that much until after he dug the bullet out.

Naturally when the doctor came he gave me a shot in the knee and took [the bullet] out. I bet it didn't take five minutes. He just made a little incision in the front, took it out, threw it in a little pail, and gave it to me. He gave me a bottle of morphine pills, which I was very happy to get. (laughs) But still no pain, now. I mean *no* pain. Well naturally they shot the knee up.

The pain came that night when the needle wore off. It felt like somebody smashed my knee with a sledgehammer. I've never had pain like that in my life, that's how much it hurt. And naturally I started taking these pills. The pills were good, so I took more than necessary. (laughs) After two weeks of that, he'd given me a bottle of a hundred pills, I went to my doctor down here. I foolishly brought the pills with me, showed him, and he immediately grabbed them and took them away from me.

Basically, that was it. No other real problems. I was sore for a month, but I was very fortunate. It hit on the side of the knee, and because it went through the rivet on the holster, and the holster itself, it slowed down enough and it hit at such an angle that it just went under the kneecap, like it skidded 'round, and it didn't do any other damage. No loss of anything, no pain, don't feel pain in it or anything like that, no problems.

But I learned a serious lesson. We fooled around. I let go a lot of things. I'd been taught by my father how to use guns, and we screwed around, pointing them at each other and doing stupid things the whole time we were there. Once you get shot, you learn a new respect.

I take it completely seriously now. I mean, I still have a lot of fun, I still own guns and stuff, but it wakes you up. The doctor told me at the hospital that if it had been a .45 I'd have had no leg. From the knee down would have been removed. But because it was a .22 . . . and we were using cheap ammo, not hollow points, no hot-load .22s, just stuff we were buying for five dollars a box because we were shooting anything and everything.

It taught me a lot of respect for guns. Needless to say, I don't shoot with that person anymore. I was raised with [guns] and I made stupid mistakes, and that's why I ended up getting shot. As much as it was his fault, it was my fault for being in that position. Up until that point . . . him taking the gun out of the holster and going, *"Fuck you, I'll shoot you"* . . . you're arguing, you're half crocked . . . just jokes. You're a kid and you don't even think. You think it's funny, "Yeah, screw you, yeah, I'll shoot you." And so you get shot. I can laugh at it now, because nothing is wrong with me from it.

All I did was learn. I laugh at it, but when I get a gun in my hand, or I'm with somebody that has a gun, there's no fooling around. I'm very watchful.

An excellent poker player, Pat Delehanty is married, has three children, and lives in northern New Jersey.

▪ FRANKIE L.

Well, I've been whacked twice, different times. Once in
Vietnam. Did you see the movie *Platoon?* I was there, in real
life. We knew they were coming, they ran right over the top
of us. We knew it, you know? I didn't know I was going to
make it out that night, but I made it. We got hit with shrapnel, mostly, but they bayonetted a couple guys and they shot
this guy Dale _____ twice in the head with an AK-47. He's
still living, to this day. Both the bullets went through the
steel part into the helmet liner and stuck right here [tem-
ple]. They broke the skin right here, and he bled. They bayonetted him just once and they took his watch and they
couldn't get his ring off but they moved on.

I got hit with shrapnel here [above the left eye] and just
bled this way [across face]. They bayonetted everybody, you
know, but they just left me alone, just left me out there.

Then the other, the second time, after I came back from
Vietnam, I was in a restaurant/bar, something like this. A
guy was there . . . it was regular people, on Northern Boulevard and Roosevelt Avenue [Queens, New York]. The guy
walked to the bathroom and I was aware, I mean, you *know,*
when somebody looks at you, like staring at you. He came
out of the bathroom and said, "What are you staring at?"

I looked at him and he stuck his gun right here [center
belly] and I whipped around, and the gun went off here,
point-blank [left side]. It got me here, went down and hit
the bone, left-hand side, through the spleen, went across

through the stomach and the intestines, up again, up my right side, and back down again into my liver. The only thing it missed was my heart and lungs.

I hit the bar, fell down. I got back up again and was starting to go after him. I carry a gun, alright? I work for the courts. I didn't have my gun on me. When I needed my gun I didn't have it on me. I fell down anyway, from the impact. There's only so much a body can take. He kneeled on my chest and put the gun between my eyes and said, "Here's another bullet for you, motherfucker."

Somebody said, "Leave him alone, he's dying." I said, "Go ahead, you bastard." He just backed off, backed out the door. They called the cops, who found the shield in my pocket. I was semiconscious. I was pissed. I didn't go into shock.

Doctor said, "You're dying."

I said, "I know that."

It was a .25 automatic, called a "surgeon's nightmare" because it bounces all over. When I seen it, when he put it right here, I said, "Aw shit." I knew he was gonna shoot me. When I seen the gun coming up, I did nothing. Like it's not real, you know?

After I was laying in the hospital—I still didn't go into shock—I called a friend of mine and told him who did it. I didn't know the guy's name, but I knew he'd killed this guy's brother years ago. I heard the name while I was laying there. It was Bolan or some shit. It was him. They got him. They didn't get the gun, but he gave himself in. Four days later. When he found out he shot a court officer, he figured, "Well, I'm in trouble now." He didn't really care that night, because he would have killed me.

This was '72 or '74. I came back from Vietnam in '68, so it was '72. I mean, I remember it like it was yesterday. There's not one thing I'll ever forget about it. Nothing. Those movements . . . I'll tell you one thing. I never go anywhere without a gun. Nowhere.

When I was in the hospital . . . first of all, when I woke up in the hospital I was so fucked up I thought I was in Heaven. I didn't know where I was because all I could see was a bright light. I wasn't really afraid to die. It was the weirdest feeling. I never want to go through it again, the pain, the major surgery.

The light, I remember seeing it. I was at peace, I really was. I'm very dominant, I guess, in my own way. I didn't want last rites. Because I said, "I'm gonna live." There's something inside you that pulls you through, I really believe that.

The doctor told my whole family, "There's nothing more I can do. It's up to God." The doctor said, "By all rights you should be dead." He even said, "You're dying." I said, "Well, if you keep standing there, I guess I will die." I was pissed off. It's the will, I believe that.

Once you've been close, when you've been on the line, as they say, everything tastes better, life looks better, feels better. With me, I just hope it's over with. I have to go see a doctor tomorrow. See, inside you really don't heal. It takes a long time to heal. Lately I've been throwing up a lot of blood. So maybe it's not over yet, you know? I've been getting a lot of pains from in here where I got whacked, you know? I don't know what the hell this is.

[My doctor] is the one who took the bullets out of the Son of Sam [victims] on Bell Boulevard, Northern Boulevard, that disco where the guy got shot up there. The kid lost his eye and I think he killed the girl. It's funny, but the doctor goes to church a lot. I didn't know that. I'm not religious. But he goes to church, I mean, my wife says he goes there a lot. She said to him, "I didn't know you were so religious," and he said, "What, did you think I pulled these miracles off by myself?" And he was in the Korean War, in like a M.A.S.H. unit. So evidently he's good. He's gotta be good. It was a July Fourth weekend when I got it, you know? And this is the kind of doctor that comes in the hospital at five o'clock in the morning, a very dedicated guy.

I've killed before, in Vietnam, and I'd kill again. Right now, if something came down in this bar, I'd take my best shot. I might get whacked, but I'm gonna take somebody with me. That's a fact. I'm a good shot. The biggest problem is you got people in a bar . . . but if they come up here they're gonna find a badge on me and a gun on me, so they'll probably shoot me again anyway. That means I'd be waiting to go through the same fucking thing I went through years ago, so I'll take my best shot.

They didn't expect me to live. But I was just pissed off. I said, "Fuck you, I'm not dying. That's it." I knew I was hit bad because it went in and never came out. I felt that burning sensation inside and I knew I was whacked good. I knew it was hot lead. Burned like a bastard. I'll never forget that feeling. It was like the worst case of heartburn or agita or whatever you want to call it. Double that times five. I knew it cooled off, from the blood or whatever. I didn't know it was in the liver, but that's where it ended up, lodged in the liver.

I lost about thirty-five pounds in two weeks. Couldn't eat, nothing at all. Nothing. When they first started me off with yogurt, I was in my second week. The third week I signed myself out. The nurses went down for lunch and when they came back I was gone. When I put my shoes on my fuckin' shoes were too big. My pants, I shrunk, literally, like thirty-five pounds. Nothing fit. My shirt was like out to here. I was pretty muscular, but it was gone, you know? I couldn't believe my shoes didn't fit. I said, "Man, something's wrong, somebody's fucking around with my clothes."

I was bleeding internally. I mean, I was bleeding inside my mouth and so on, but not much. I knew I was bleeding inside. I started to get weak. The life was draining out of me, I knew that. I knew I was dying. When I was laying there I talked to a homicide cop, and I told my friend who did this, and I had trouble breathing, you know? I was getting clammy. I was starting to get shock. I was getting weak. When he said, "You're dying," I said, "I know that." I guess from Vietnam, from all the training I had.

That was a feeling, when you know they're coming. We got hit pretty bad, and that night we had dead all over. I fired over three thousand rounds of machine gun fire. It was in the newspapers everywhere. That night we knew they were coming again, and we heard them walking in the water. The ones that were left, there wasn't many of us left, I had a bayonet here [in one hand] and one here [other hand] and three rounds in an M16. That was it. And it was funny, I wasn't scared. I was ready.

It was some of the old Wolfhounds, a brother outfit, coming to relieve us. They expected to walk into combat, too. We were ready to go. It was them coming to relieve us. Otherwise. . . .

But I wasn't afraid, you know? We had dead all over the place. Lost a lot of guys over there. I saw a guy with his guts, he got shot across the belly and his intestines fell out. I thought the guy was gonna die. And the medic ran over and just took a canteen, washed off his intestines, put 'em on top of his belly, gave him a shot of morphine, and pulled an evac. The guy was walking around five days later. Literally walking around. Stitched up. I mean he was mobile. They took him back to a medevac hospital—and in Vietnam they were all over the place—they'd fly 'em in on choppers, and there's surgeons there and they put his intestines back in. He wasn't even hit in the intestines. Just across the front of the gut. His belly just opened up and his intestines fell out. I thought the fucking guy was dead. I said, "Aw, look at this shit." I mean, I didn't do it, I was just standing there.

Other guys lost their legs, man. One guy was in the hospital, I was talking to him, and they told me he'd be all right. But he told me he didn't feel good. And he died. Why'd he die? He had a piece of shrapnel in his jugular vein, killed him. He was in there for over a week and a half before it moved.

Shock kills so many people. Shock is really what kills you. See, in the army they train you. First of all, you're young and you don't have responsibility. I guess that's why they say youths, eighteen, nineteen, twenty, single, make the best soldiers. I would never do now what I did over there. I've got a wife and kids, you know? On the Cambodian border they told us to get up and move out. We had dead guys all around us, but we got up and moved out. As we're moving out we're saying, "What the fuck, there's a guy with a .50-caliber machine gun knocking the shit out of us but we're moving out."

Combat. I don't know anybody that's been in combat that said they'd want to go back. Yeah, you may miss the action, but . . . when you're nineteen years old, twenty years old, you're gung ho, that's one thing. But when you get to Vietnam and you smell all those body bags when you get off that plane and you see all these fuckin' bags lined up going that way with tags on 'em you *know*. You get the odor of death. You say, "Whoa, what the fuck am I doing here?" You're coming off and they're going back. They gotta get them out of there because of the heat, you know? The movie *Platoon* was almost true except for the rape bullshit. The killing was true, not that we ever killed any of our own, but the killings were real, just like that.

I've put 'em in body bags, legs, arms . . . we had a lieutenant who came out in the field. We were walking and this guy had enough brains to say, "Hey Sarge, I ain't no fucking hero, man. I wanna get back." He was a nice guy. He came out in the field, and you don't know what days are out there—he was just out there one day. He was out there that night. He was one of the few officers we had, and he was told, "Listen to these guys out there, these guys are veterans, they know their shit." You've got your red ants, snakes, everything's against you, weather, booby traps all over the place. You can't trust the people. We were walking toward a hedge berm through a rice paddy, and it just don't look right, you know? I had my RTO, I said, "Tell 'em, this is double oh three five, tell 'em it's not right. Something's wrong up there. I don't like it."

We all spread out walking, I guess everybody felt the same way, you get a feeling after a while. I was ready to hit the ground, and they opened up on us. This guy was to my left, at a 45 degree angle, and I was yelling, "Stay down, *stay the fuck down.*" And before I knew it he gets up on one knee, takes a grenade out, and goes like this [cocks arm back to throw overhand]. He caught a burst from an AK-47 across the chest and it blew him backward and he landed on the grenade. Next thing I know, *booff*, it was all over. Blew him right in half. You know, we called in artillery and we killed a few of 'em, but most of 'em probably got away.

When I got over to him it was like looking at a side of beef, man you could see the ribs. I felt so bad, this guy's been out in the field not thirty hours. From here [waist] up was one piece, and from here down was another. I couldn't believe it. I said, "Why didn't he just stay the fuck down?" His intentions were probably very honorable, but when you get a burst across the fuckin' chest, that's bad enough. That probably killed him. I guess he must have realized if he wasn't dead, that he was laying on top of a grenade, you know? He must have said, "Aw shit . . ." I don't know what went through his head.

Every once in a while I think about that shit, you know? These things come back to me. There's some things that don't leave your mind. This guy M_____: when I went down to the Wall in Washington, the book was there, it's a big thick book of all the names on the Wall. I was there for the opening of the Memorial. I flew down. I just felt I was drawn there. So I was standing there and I was talking to this CIA agent. I had to use my shield to get in, they said you needed a press pass or a pass, I said, "Fuck that . . ." so the guy said, "Come on." I was just thinking of M_____, and the pages of the book blew. It stopped at a page and the first name at the top of the page was M_____. He was a sergeant. He was screaming, he got hit. I said, "Stop screaming, you sound like a fucking faggot. Stop, man. You're one of the guys from New York, knock it off." He said, "Naw, no, I'm gonna die . . ." I said, "You're not gonna die so stop it. You sound like a fucking cunt, you know?" They hit him with morphine.

He was saying, "I'm not gonna make it. My mother don't know I'm over here . . ." He died about five minutes later. I felt bad, you know?

These things just come back. You think about these guys who got whacked. Two guys were screaming, I stayed with them all night, I wouldn't leave them. They were on one side, and I was on the other side. The VC couldn't come down because I had an M60 machine gun and everybody that came down I could kill. I kept shooting the ones that were coming down. I told these guys, "Chill, man, I'm right here, I ain't going nowhere, don't worry." I told 'em, "You sound like a bunch of fucking faggots over there." Trying to humor them, you know? Keep 'em from going into shock. It got quiet and I said, "You guys all right?" They said, "Yeah yeah yeah." I said, "You want some cocktails over there?" I was gonna throw some morphine over there. I threw it, I don't know if they got it.

The VC pulled back and I stayed. They couldn't get me out either. I wouldn't leave them. They were throwing rifle grenades at me, everything, but they couldn't come down. I got a good body count. But those two guys died.

These memories, you know? When you're sleeping you can hear every word. I don't know if it's subconscious. There's some things you can never, never forget.

Another guy, he got whacked, he was a tough little bastard. His name was Rodney, they called him "Super Egg." He used to cut their ears off. He got it, man. When you hear these guys scream, you know, when you're sleeping your subconscious picks up every word. I don't know why it does that to you. But it's just like yesterday. My kids wake me up sometimes. I'm soaking wet. And then I don't remember, but I'm talking in my sleep, "*Stay down.*"

My experience with communism is when we came across a village and there's kids there. We gave the kids chocolate bars and peaches, whatever it was. Maybe cigarettes, because the little kids run around with cigarettes in their mouths. They were nice to us. The VC came and cut all the babies' heads off and stuck them on bamboo poles. One day these kids, I'd seen them three or four times; hello, you know, you're nice to them. A kid is a kid, you're attracted to a child. Next time you see him his head's on a bamboo pole. To me, that's communism.

I'll never forget that. I don't give a fuck, if a guy's a commie, I think, "Just kill him." Fuck it. That's communism to me. I've seen it in its worst form, but hey, kill it before it grows, that's my philosophy.

Frankie L. is an officer of the Supreme Court of the State of New York.

■ STEVE MALINCHOC

The biggest reaction I had to getting shot was the shock and the burning of the hot bullet. What happened was, my ex-wife, at that time we were still married but she was dating this guy, and this guy was a corrections officer. Every weekend I had visitation rights for the kids so I would drive up there early in the morning and pick them up on Saturday. At this time my daughter was at a party, so we're all milling around.

We got along reasonably well, but this guy had a real macho image problem. He'd always make big stories to my son, because my son lived up there at that time. This guy would make up these big stories with Peter, and he could carry a gun when he was on the job. So here we are, all milling around with a whole bunch of kids, in this big complex, housing complex, and this guy's playing with a .22-caliber derringer. Double-barreled, you know, one of these things a woman would carry. And he's putting bullets in it.

Now, if you pulled a knife out and started cleaning your nails, you're an adult, and I wouldn't tell you, "Hey, look, be careful, you're gonna cut yourself." I figure the guy knows what he's doing. He's an adult, right? He's not gonna shoot anybody, right?

So everybody mills around. This is like early morning, there's dozens of little kids. I had a brand new automobile, I mean literally brand new. My kid was sitting in the car and I was standing next to the car. I hear this loud noise, and I get flung around. And I feel this burning sensation in my back, really burning. I didn't know what it was, but when I turned around this guy was like a river of blood. He was fiddling with the gun with his hand over the barrel, as you would hold a little tiny derringer, right? And I guess it was cocked, he was trying to unload it, and his finger slipped off the thing and it went right through his hand, bounced off his bone, and ricocheted into my back. I was talking to a little kid whose head was right at the level where the bullet went in. It could have killed the kid.

I turned around. I didn't know what had happened, I didn't know I was shot at that moment. Well, it was like pushing a button and animating everybody in the whole area. Everybody got all bent out of shape, you know? This guy had shot himself, I guess there's a main artery but I don't know. I look on the ground and there's a puddle of blood and it's getting bigger. The blood is spurting out of his hand, like a little fountain.

So they jump into their car. This is upstate in Peekskill. They know where the hospital is and I don't. My wife gets me into the car and we're driving to the hospital. By the time we get to the hospital they've arrested him for possession of the gun. He lost his job for like six months.

They put me on the table and they took X-rays. They said, "You're not in any danger so we're not gonna take the bullet out until we get a bunch of doctors in here who have never seen gunshot wounds."

Well, it was nothing, because I'm fat as a pig and it went in the side and just went in about this far [four inches]. So what they did, they gave me a shot and said, "Look, if it wears off, tell us." It was no more than an hour and a half and they've got a flock of doctors in there. All they did was put a knife in and cut along the hole until they got to the bullet and they took it out. So it was no big deal.

I guess you're disappointed that I didn't have my balls shot off or something; *Yes, I have a wooden ball.* (laughs) But of course I was in the papers, the *Daily News* and the *Post*, and they mentioned my name five times and spelled it different five times. They never spelled it right.

They fixed his hand up and they sent him to jail. He had

to post a few thousand dollars' bond to get out. This was a Saturday morning, and they made me stay overnight, and for some reason they made me stay over another night. Then they were really gonna give me the works, like Monday morning they wanted to take five thousand blood tests and every other thing. I said, "Hey I'm getting out of here." Because there was nothing wrong with me. They told me there was nothing wrong with me, that all I would do was get a little bit of pain. But there was no pain. There wasn't. They stitched me up and I was fine. My wife took the stitches out. I didn't even bother going back.

The best thing was, I had this brand new Ferrari, a twelve-cylinder. It was a beautiful dark-blue color with this bone-colored interior. They gave me a towel. And my wife is getting a little, not panicked, but she doesn't know how to get to the hospital. This guy's bleeding like a pig, and they know all the roads, and they're going through red lights and around traffic and everything. My wife can drive like a mad-woman, but she doesn't know where they're actually going. And I'm asking her, "Hey, am I bleeding on the seats?"

The most interesting thing about it is, when you're in this kind of business, like the quote "art business," or you're on a vacation that's reasonably posh, to use that term, like a cruise. We go on a lot of cruises. And somebody will mention bullets or shooting or something like that. And you say, "Oh, you know I was shot," and they'll look at you like it's a disease. Like it's antisocial behavior if you got shot. Never mind what the reason was. And of course the story I told you doesn't have the connotations that it does when you tell somebody, "My ex-wife's boyfriend shot me." They instantly think, "Oh boy, this is a juicy tale of catching 'em in the sack or something like that."

Steve Malinchoc owns a thriving graphic arts business in New York, serving music industry clients.

■ HORACIO

In 1970, there was in Chile a big movement of people trying to elect Allende. Allende was the candidate from the socialist parties in Chile. The political organization, especially the organization around the working class people, was very strong, for so many years, and they came to the point where it was possible to elect a socialist president. There was so much support, so many people. Even part of the middle class in Chile was supporting Allende at this moment.

The reason why is in the whole history of this huge political movement, but also because the rich classes in Chile were divided about how to confront the election, what is going to happen next, how they can solve the crisis—because Chile was having an economic crisis. For these reasons, we come to 1970 with Allende. He was a socialist. The group, the coalition behind him, wasn't. It was different parties, a pluralistic group, but with huge, huge support from the people. On the other side we have these rich classes dividing into different parties, with no clear strategy about how to confront the election.

Allende won in 1970. This created possibilities for the political organization, the socialist organization, the revolutionary organization, and all the advocates for housing and whatever to try to develop so many plans throughout Chile.

I found myself doing a lot of political work with one of the revolutionary organizations, concentrating my work in housing. My work actually was to build and develop political consciousness and organize homeless people to build a coalition of homeless people, but also to pressure the Allende government to go farther and farther and really take the power in Chile. With Allende we took part of the power, but we didn't really take full power. The army was controlled by the rich classes, and the distribution system was controlled by the rich classes also. Allende was trying to do something, but not too much.

The huge mobilization of the mass movement created the normal reaction. The rich classes got together and said, "Okay, we fucked up in '70, now we have to push the army to do a coup." The coup happened in 1973.

In 1973, all the people involved in politics were persecuted. During the three years of the Allende government I did political roundhousing. I traveled. I was considered at that moment one of the persons that the military dictatorship wanted in jail. They started to look for me, like they started to look for *so* many, many other activists and people involved in whatever.

I went underground. I lived until September 1974 in the underground, changing from place to place, trying to avoid the army and the secret police. Many of the people that worked with me in the political movement were killed, or they went to jail, they went to concentration camps, they were tortured, et cetera. It was difficult to live in the underground, it was very risky, but we knew that the only possible way to survive was to keep living underground. If the worst situation comes, if the police come, maybe you have to confront the police with weapons. Self-defense.

In September '74, after a year or so of living underground, most of the people working with me, around me, started to get caught by the police. We tried to strengthen the security measures, how to live, how to move, but that was the worst moment for the political organization in Chile. Everyone was under siege. It was really, really bad. We didn't have money, we didn't have support, we didn't have a house to live in.

At the same time the secret police were looking for me they were looking for my family. Through them to get to me. They were watching them, waiting. In '74 my mother decided to change houses because the risk to be caught by the police and tortured was increasing and was really, really bad. Many people that she and I knew were cooperating with the secret police. In order for them to save their lives they were saying things. My mother decided to move. When she moved, the people who were watching her house got crazy, because it was possible she might lead them to where I was. And they followed her. On the way to the new house she stopped at my apartment to leave some furniture. The police discovered the place where I was.

They waited until the night. Around eleven o'clock they came to my house, the apartment where I was living, on the fourth floor, and at the same time they went to my mother's house, and to my son's mother's house.

In the apartment where I was living, they caught me there. And I thought it was a terrible mistake . . . you never believe these things happen. There was a knock at the door, and I had just finished dinner with two ladies that lived across the hallway. I thought the ladies were coming back to pick up their cigarettes or whatever they left. I opened the door, and there was the secret police.

They hit me so badly, immediately they threw me to the floor, and started to hit me so badly on my face and all over my body. They took my son's mother also, who was with me, they took her to the bathroom and tortured her there. They started to torture me in the bedroom. They asked me questions, who else was living there, where were the arms and the weapons, who are the contact people, the more important people in the resistance, and all this kind of stuff.

I kept saying, "No, nobody lives here." There was a couple of things in my house, I had a couple of very important weapons in my house at this time, and I said, "Nobody lives here, this is a place where we store weapons. That's why nobody knows about this place."

That was my answer. Shit, I couldn't say who else I know, because they'll go after them. All this happened until about twelve o'clock; an hour, two hours, something like that. From there, they made us put some clothes on, and they took us to the torture houses. They covered our eyes and threw us into a truck.

They took us to a house, and took me to a basement, both of us, and they started to torture us. On the level, they almost killed us. They did everything. They put the electricity all over your body. They tie you on a metal table, and there's two or three guys for each table. You're tied all over, completely naked, and they put the electricity in your anus, your penis, your eyes. That's probably the worst, the eyes.

You lose consciousness. Every five minutes you are out, and this fucking doctor comes to you and they start to beat you up to make you react. It's fucking crazy.

There was more people there. You can't see anybody, but you can feel them and hear the screams. They violate every single woman, they rape every single woman in there. They kept doing this shit, and they kept putting this stuff in my body, like drugs or something, to make me talk. Around probably five o'clock in the morning, I was keeping to my story about nobody's going to come to my house, this is a storage place, I really don't have too much connection with nobody, I was in charge of those weapons.

About five o'clock, after being out so many times, my body didn't respond anymore and my mind was completely crazy. This feeling of isolation and fear . . . the fear is the worst. It's a feeling that I never had in my life before. They are hunters, and you are the hunted, and there is *nothing* you can do.

Out of this desperation, I said, "Yes, people are going to come to my house." In order to stop that, to give them something to stop this shit. They started to question me; I said, "Yes, somebody is going to come, he's going to come this morning, and he's an important person." The problem was, I knew it wasn't true. Nobody's going to this house. Nobody knew this house. But I had to say something to stop them.

They said, "Okay, if this is true, we're going to take you there." They put me in clothes again, I was naked the whole night. I was completely . . . my body was shit. They broke one of my kidneys around here, they broke a couple of ribs, because they beat me, beat me, beat me up before they did all this electricity stuff. I couldn't walk, almost. They gave me my clothes, that were pieces of shit now, and they threw me into this car and we drove to my apartment. Ten people from the security command went upstairs with walkie-talkies and all this stuff, to wait for the people that were going to come to the house.

I was downstairs in the car with one of the officers and this bodyguard. My role was to identify the people when they were coming to the house, to alert the people upstairs. They would have to go four stories up, and on the way they would catch them.

We waited, and that was crazy, because I knew nobody's going to come. They were terrifying me. I was so fucking scared my whole body was trembling so much, I could not control my bowels. I could not control anything. I was tired, but this was such a shocking situation that my eyes were like that [wide open] . . . but those guys, they were tired also. It was incredible. In one moment these guys start to kind of [nod] like they were going to sleep. I thought, "Shit, I have to escape this shit."

My mind started to go around; how am I going to do that? I think, "If those guys go to sleep and I hit one and try to take the gun from the other, I can do something." There were no handcuffs, because I couldn't move. They put me like that and I stayed like that. That saved my life.

The driver was [shows arm across the back of the seat, relaxed] and he had his gun here [under left armpit]. The bodyguard was in the backseat with me and he kept his gun under here, under his leg.

I was watching, watching . . . but to make the fucking decision, man, I didn't have the courage to make the decision. I was so scared, like never in my life. But I was thinking, thinking, thinking.

Suddenly, seven o'clock in the morning, the guys started to wake up. We were there for an hour and a half, two hours. Nothing had happened. These guys started to terrify me, saying, "Listen motherfucker, if this isn't true, what happened last night is nothing to what's going to happen to you."

When he said that I knew, I *knew*, that they were going to kill me. Like they killed every single one of my friends. I got so . . . like in a shock situation, like a shock state.

The guy who was by my side, the bodyguard . . . at the corner where the car was there was a bakery. They were open, the bakery, just at this moment. He said to the other guy, "Listen, I'm gonna go out and buy some bread." The guy said, "Yes." So he opened the door, he went out, he ran to the bakery.

I'm in this situation, man, it's now or never. There was a pen in the backseat. I took the pen and hit the motherfucker officer in one eye. I put the whole pen in his eye.

All this shit was like *prowf* . . . the window was like, oh shit, it was crazy, man. Even like that, this guy took his gun out and he started to scream. He started to say, "You blew it, motherfucker, you blew it."

That made me, oh, that made me more crazy, and I jumped over him and started to bite him on the face, hitting him, whatever. I never was able to take the gun away from him because he was in shock, nervous shock. But because of that he was unable to shoot. I opened the door and he grabbed me with his other hand, grabbed my jacket. I tried to walk out but he had grabbed me, and he couldn't open, he couldn't close, he was in shock. Whatever was in his hand was going to stay forever there.

I took my jacket off of me and fell down out of the car, and I tried to walk. This guy is screaming, he's *screaming*, man. I started to walk a little like that, tried to cross the street, and the other guy came out of the bakery.

I didn't care. I couldn't care, I just walked. And this guy fucking shot me, *blauw blauw blauw*, and one of the bullets passed through my leg. It didn't really hurt me, but it touched part of my testicle and my leg. I fell down, but I quick got up again and kept walking. I kept walking. I didn't know what had happened, my mind was blank. I didn't feel pain, I didn't feel anything.

This goddamnit, this guy, he never came after me. Probably he saw this spectacle, it was terrifying, this scene there, or he went to get some help for the guy, I don't know.

But I walked. I went to this building, got into the court-yard, there was a complex like this, got in there with my mind totally blank. I went to the third floor, second floor, third floor, fifth floor . . . what do I do now? I was thinking maybe I could knock on a door or something, but I found in those old buildings, you can go to the . . . between the roof and the last apartment there is a place. You can sometimes go in there, there is a water tank and all this stuff. I got into there, and there was this tank, and I was trying to hide myself so I went in, and I fell into this fucking tank.

There was almost no water, just like this [six inches] but I almost drowned myself. I lost consciousness for three hours or so. When I woke up my body was shivering and I had fever, very bad fever. And I felt the pain in my body, I felt the pain of everything all over. It was terrifying. I didn't want to move one inch from there. I was still in a shock situation. For that reason I didn't think anything about . . . if I was carrying a gun at that moment I probably would have shot myself. Because I was in shock. What was clear in my mind was that I could not, for one second again, be in the hands of those people. The only thing I wanted at that moment was to get a gun and have it with me. I waited maybe two more hours without moving, trying to think what I was going to do. I was going to go to this house, maybe they can help me, I can clean myself.

I walked out of the building, it was almost night, and I took a taxi to this house. The people almost fainted when they saw me because I was in such terrible shape. I asked for money, and I asked for new clothes, and I left the house because they said no, they can't keep me there. They were terrified. I went to another house. They took me, and I went to a kind of emergency underground hospital, clinic, whatever. I spent three months there, almost without moving, with a gun under my pillow every night. And a grenade. And I said, "If those people come here I'm gonna blow my head off, because I don't want to live in a situation like that."

At the same time, these other things were passing through my mind. I was building a feeling about how fucking much I want to live, man. Shit. I want to live so much. Not for just one minute, but I want to live for so *long*.

There were two things that probably made me so strong. Saying I'm willing to lose everything, to blow my head off if those guys, the military dictatorship, steps here in this house. I was willing to do that, to end my life. On the other side what I was getting was a reaction that what I did was right, that this is the way I want to build my life. This is the way I want to live. And if I can live this way, I want to live for *so long*. And I got this incredible feeling. My whole life was passing, every single minute that I was unable to sleep. I didn't sleep for three months. Every single night I was awake. The only time I could sleep was in the day because I knew there was people in the house. I was terrified about the silence, and about night . . . I spent three months watching out of the window, with a gun in my hand, waiting for something. Shit. Waiting for anything.

In this period, in this process, this incredible need to live and enjoy every single minute was building in me with such strength. In some ways it was probably an incredible help in terms of . . . I had to assume the new situations that were happening so fast in front of me in my life.

After three months in this house I started to go out again, started to do new political work; *very* underground kind of stuff, very little, because the whole fucking military army was behind me. To go outside on the street was a huge process, I mean, shit . . .

You can choose about everything. You can choose, and you keep going. In March '75 the situation of this political organization was completely destroyed. I said, "Okay, I have to move out of the country. I cannot survive here. They are going to take me any minute." I was going from one house to another house, and the police were coming behind me just a day away. It came to the moment when I had to get out of the country, and the International Red Cross, they got me out of the country and I went to Costa Rica. And the first thing I did in Costa Rica was to go to the beach.

I went to one of those incredible, beautiful beaches with nobody there. Just nature. And I realized that all this shit I have in my mind, in my body . . . this moment was like *prawf*, I threw it out of there. Nature was, for me at that moment, the best therapy. This beautiful country, and the sun, was the best I can get. The best therapy. I started to rebuild again, the whole mind, the whole body, myself. What am I going to do now? How am I gonna go? How am I going to carry all this shit with me and transform all of this stuff into something. . . .

This was such a strong feeling that I developed during the days of torture and living underground, a strong feeling about life that made me initiate new perspectives, develop new projects, and go ahead and say, "Okay, from now on, a new life."

Horacio is alive and well in the Western Hemisphere.

■ CRAZY ACE

It was down in San Luis Obispo. I was going out with this girl, who was a junkie I guess, that's the best way to describe her. I dropped her off, she wanted to see some friends, and she told me, "Come down this alley and knock on the door, and I'll be ready for you."

Well, I was lucky inasmuch as the alley was a dead-end alley, but there was like a T right before. She'd set me up; they were gonna shoot me and take my motorcycle. The guy with the gun out in the alley was a little trigger-happy. The first bullet hit me in the right hand, right at the base of the thumb, and knocked my hand off the handlebar.

I really didn't realize what it was because it didn't hurt. It was more like a roach or a kamikaze bug hittin' you, you know, when you're going down the highway real fast and big bugs hit you. It was kinda like that, and it knocked my hand off the handlebars and I kind of shook my hand and reached up to the handlebars again and blood was running down my hand. All of a sudden *bang*, I got hit right there on my other hand. They were shooting at my head, but I had big high pullback handlebars and instead it hit me in both hands. When I realized what it was, that somebody was shooting at me, I wasn't into the dead end yet, and I swung down the alley and got away.

The one bullet went in there and just tore the skin out. The other one went in and hit me here, you can see the scar on this one, hit me in there and just lodged right in the bone. Didn't even break the bone. Twenty-two caliber soft-nosed shells. If they'd have hit me with a hard-nosed shell it would have ricocheted all over the place and done all kinds of damage. And fortunately they were lousy shots. They were shooting at my head.

To me it was like, it wasn't painful. I dug the bullet out with a pocket knife, didn't go to the hospital, didn't go to the doctor about it. There was no bones broken, there wasn't any severe damage, so I figured, why should I waste my money and go through all the hassle with the cops and everything else, you know?

I got *stabbed* in the chest. I had my throat cut. They missed my vein, when they went to cut my throat I went back and they cut me right across the chin. Of course, the blood was all the same, all the blood gushed right straight down and they didn't know they hadn't cut my throat and they threw me on the road and left me there. I wasn't gonna yell at 'em, "Hey stupid," you know?

The thing in the chest was a stab wound. A guy buried a Buck knife in my chest. The knife went in and hit my rib, and the blade turned sideways and slipped between my lung and my diaphragm. . . . I beat the guy up before I even went to the hospital. I went to the hospital and got six stitches, all these X-rays and stuff, and if the hospital just left it alone it would have healed a lot faster because when they closed it up they didn't stop all the bleeding on the inside. There was a big lump in my chest, a big hard lump of black, half-congealed blood. For like four, five days afterwards.

I took an X-Acto knife and autoclaved it. Cut it open, drained it, put a wick in it, and didn't have any more problems. I did a better job than the hospital does.

Crazy Ace is a tattoo artist, photographer, author, and actor who currently lives and works in Richmond, Virginia.

■ HARLEY SWIFTDEER

A conversation between Chris Pfouts and Harley Swiftdeer.

HS: I've been shot a total of four times. Being shot is not fun. And it's a lot different, too. I've been hit once, well, not really as a civilian but as a Texas highway patrolman, and the rest of it was in 'Nam, so there's different kinds of situations. Also I've got shrapnel all through my back. That's a whole different issue. In fact, it'll sound stupid, but you talk to almost any vet who's been hit hard, and he'll take a gunshot wound over shrapnel any day of the week.

CP: Yeah, I have a friend who was a marine and he got shrapnel in the legs. When I first got shot I called him and said, "What about this pain?" Because if you haven't had any heavy pain, it takes a long time to figure out how to deal with it.

HS: Especially because it's pain that just penetrates, it goes from throbbing to piercing, from piercing to throbbing, and it won't go away. You can't move into it like you can with other types of pain. It's different. That's where most people lose it. That's why so many guys from over here came out dopeheads, because they can't regulate it with anything but painkillers, and of course if you try that you're screwed. Especially if it's really severe wounds. It depends on where you were hit. Gut wounds are the hardest. I'd almost rather get shot anywhere but the head or the gut. Anywhere else, it's a lot better. . . .

CP: My friend has a lot of things to say about pain . . . he has arthritis, too. It worked out pretty well, because whatever worked for him didn't work for me. What works for arthritis doesn't work for what I got. That eliminates a whole field of treatment.

HS: How long has it been since you got hit?

CP: About a year and a half.

HS: You still have pain with it?

CP: Yeah. Oh yeah.

HS: Okay, that's literally the pain tape, or the aftershock memory. You can get rid of that. But you've got to do it the way I do it, the shamanic way. You can't do it the doctor way, it won't work.

CP: I know that. I haven't been to a doctor yet that knows anything about pain. Even the pain clinic people don't know anything about pain. I don't think they ever had any, is the problem.

HS: (laughs)

CP: It's funny but it's true. There's a difference between having a headache and real pain.

HS: See, they don't know, Chris, how to deal with post traumatic shock syndrome, because that's really what you're dealing with. You're dealing with the fact that when you get hit, there is a trauma. But yet you've still got to function. Because of that, your body encodes the shock trauma, and it's shock trauma at the end that. . . . All pain is is a signal that there is something that's out of balance. Pain is a signal. It's like a fire alarm. Real quick analogy, see if this makes sense to you: If all of a sudden a fire alarm goes off here, we don't sit around drinking our Dr. Peppers, and I don't go over and cut off the alarm so we can finish our conversation. Nor do I go over and stuff pillows around it to get it to shut up. And I don't cut the wires. I go find out why the goddamn alarm went off.

Doctors cut the alarm; that's surgery. Or they'll stuff pillows around it; that's medication. Or they'll shut it off, which is long, extended treatment. That's the three methodologies that medical practice uses, none of which acknowledge what pain is. Pain is a signal that must be acknowledged, that you know your body has been put into a traumatic state, therefore you have to change whatever the cause was for the effect of the trauma.

You have to change the cause, or the effect of the trauma will stay. The pain signal keeps broadcasting until you shut off the signal at the cause, and that's the trauma itself. So you've got to literally remove the trauma from the spirit, if you will, of the person. Remove it from the mental space of the person, so that they will no longer broadcast that signal. That's why it stays. How often do you see yours come up when you're under a lot of stress?

CP: Sure it's stress-related. I live in New York City, where stress is more a part of daily life than it is in other places. I'll tell you what I did for it, and I know it won't sound as screwy to you as it does to some people, but I bought another femur. I bought a specimen femur and I keep it in a drawer. Using your same analogy of fire, I just think, well, there is a fire, but I want it to burn over there, in that other femur.

HS: What you're doing is displacing the pain, which'll work. What I do, I teach people; that's why we do it in the sweat lodge, you literally go back in, right back through the trauma. You rebirth it. Then you accept that signal and you give it away, the same as placing it in the bone. You could bring the femur and I could place it all in there and then it's done. But you've got to know how to do it shamanically. See, it's energy. People don't understand, everything's energy. There's nothing mystical or mysterious about magic or shamanism; it's basic laws, but it's laws that don't function in the third dimension the way we experience things. It operates in the fifth dimension. But it works. I've done it for too damn many veterans not to know it works. And for police officers, people who get shot, or get hurt, or get real heavy-duty trauma. It could even be an accident victim.

CP: I'm kind of a philistine by nature, but following a trauma like that you will look for relief in places other than where you sit. You have to.

HS: In anything that can happen, there's a 20 percent possibility of chance. So, one of two things: either you chose to get shot as a way of teaching yourself about something, which means you're in the 80 percent. Or it was just pure chance. One of the first things you have to do is find out if it was chance or pattern. That's critical in the recovery stages.

It's really interesting, the first time I got shot was in 1960, right at the end of my first tour of duty in 'Nam. That's when I got this one here in my arm, this pucker scar right here. It hit, chipped the bone, and came out the exit side over here. It was just a simple thing. It was in the middle of a firefight. We were on routine patrol, because at that time I was over there as just a military advisor. My primary function was training regular Vietnamese army to fight, and they didn't want to fight. I don't want to get into that, but we came down under a firefight condition and they started running.

Which sucks. (laughs) I mean, they're supposed to be your support system and you look around and these guys have bulldogged it back the other way, and you go, "Screw this shit . . ." When I saw that I turned this way and it came across. And it stung like a sonofabitch. The first imprint was this burning, stinging sensation, and then the realization in my brain, because everything went into real slow motion, in my brain it said: You've been hit.

I looked down and saw my torn fatigues, and blood, and I did this [flex] . . . I had my weapon in my right hand, the hand works, and I said, "Well, it ain't bad." I kept everything going on semiautonomic, just phased it out, but *boy* . . . it's hard to judge time, probably an hour, an hour and a half later, *whoa!* Boy, the pain was through my whole body. It would resonate from here, but I could not get that piercing-type burn sensation out of my head and out of my energy field. God, it just. . . . Then I got back and it was a good three to five hours before I really got it treated, per se, and by this time the pain is just overbearing. And you know it hurt for about two years, just kept coming back under weird conditions.

There's no metal left in the body on that one, it's just a clean wound, what they call a superficial. Just chipped a bone and of course didn't hit any arteries. It's literally what they call a "forty-eight and out" injury over there, you know forty-eight hours and you're back in combat again. I got a Purple Heart, big fuckin' deal.

That one wasn't traumatic. The second time I got hit was in the leg, and that was. That was on the inside of the left thigh.

Again, thank God, it didn't hit any major bone. It missed the bone by five-sixteenths of an inch or something. Sometimes I think, well, that would have got me home, I wouldn't have had to go back again. (laughs) That one . . . I almost lost consciousness with that one, because it was really severe. It was also in a firefight, but this time we were down, defensive, perimeter.

I don't really know how it happened. I just know I got hit, I don't know where it came from. I don't even know. It was a night and . . . I got all that out of my head. See, I lost consciousness in there, because I can't remember exactly when it happened. But boy, the pain from that lasted for about four years. I would wake up at night with my leg going tight, locking, like when you get a bad muscle cramp, but with this burning sensation going all the way up and into my jaws. My jaws would start to lock. I couldn't figure what that one was all about. The only thing I've been able to trace it back to is I lost two really good friends that were on either side of me. Somewhere in all of that is when I got hit. There's other stuff overlaid on it, so I never have been able to figure it out.

That one . . . there was so much blood loss that I had to tie it off up here, and the corpsmen came in of course and gave me morphine and sulfa packs and took me out on a helicopter. That was nice because I got to go back to the

Philippines for a little R&R. It was sweet. But the pain from that was just awesome. I'd wake up and my leg was almost in a rigor mortis lock, my whole body trembling and sweating, God dang, sweat would just pour off me.

That one really fucking hurt. That was the worst one. Other than the shrapnel, that was the most severe pain that I've ever been through.

The third one . . . well actually, the fourth one was the one that sent me home, and that got me a metal plate up here [on top of head] and pins in both knees, and that was getting blown out of a helicopter. That was a mortar round, a one five five. I was standing in the door, getting guys out, and the next thing I knew, and this is the weirdest thing that ever happened to me, next thing I know, this is hard to even talk about, I'm *above* the helicopter and I'm watching my body go whupsy-doozy, two and a half twists, you know, rated nine on the grading scale, right into the ground, and the rest of the guys coming out of the chopper and fanning out, and boy, heavy, heavy fire, and the medics running up. I'm watching the whole scene from above, and I'm thinking, "Hey, this is cool, it's really cool." There was no pain, no shock; I was *completely* out of my body. It was the first really strong, focused out-of-body experience I ever had.

The firefight was going on around, and there was heavy, heavy loss on our part. We walked right into something we didn't know was there. Next thing I know they're coming in and they're putting my body into this frigging wicker basket. As it went up it started spinning, and I got dizzy as shit, and I'm thinking, "How could I be looking at this and getting dizzy," and then I became aware of the fact that I wasn't in my body. And then all of a sudden, boy, there was this blinding flash of just awesome pain in my head, 'cause I looked at my face and my eyes were open . . . holy shit, the terror of that, I still can't get that out of my mind.

I thought they were going to leave without me. (laughs) Which I guess sounds stupid as shit, but I thought they were, and I said, "They can't leave without me." And boom, boy, it was instant darkness.

As a result of that I was in a coma for forty-eight days. During that length of time my heartbeat stopped three times. I almost bought it on that. Real interesting. I had some real strong going-down-the-tunnel-type feelings, out into a big field of lights . . . something just made me realize it wasn't time to leave then, that I have a choice about when I leave. That was important. And I just didn't go. That was a pretty hard hit.

CP: We had talked about this with another guy, that . . . when I had lost so much blood . . . I got shot on the corner, got up, walked home, climbed a flight of stairs and dialed 911 and told 'em to come get my sorry ass. I'd still love to hear that tape. I'd just moved into the place and it was all I could do to remember the house number . . .

HS: See, that's what I mean by autonomic. You do whatever you've got to do.

CP: Oh yeah, there's a whole lot going on there. But then I called someone else to double it up, told them to call 911 for me and make sure that I'd really done it, and then call me back and talk to me while I'm waiting. I guess I must have tied something around my leg, I can't remember doing it but there's a real good chance I'd be dead if I hadn't. . . .

HS: See, it's all that stuff you did, I'm convinced, because I've seen so much of it, especially with vets, that *that's* what produces the afterpain when there shouldn't quote unquote really physiologically be any. That's why medical doctors don't know what to do about it. They say, "Look, all the stuff's healed, there should be no more pain." But it's in that period between when you get hit and when you finally get treated, for lack of a better word . . . that period in there, you've gotta function on autonomic. That's my theory. I mean it's obviously a fucking theory.

CP: It's as good as anything modern medicine has to offer. I thought, and I still think, the pain is just one long scream from there. It's been insulted and it's not happy about it.

HS: Exactly. Until you acknowledge what that was giving you, what the payback was for . . . I know that sounds silly as shit, but there is a *fucking* payback. Anything any of us have ever done we're doing for some frigging reason. And there's a payback. Pain is one of the ways we acknowledge that we're on this fucking planet. When you're in pain you *know* you're here. (laughs) You *know* you're here. And it's like a signal, and again, this is just me and my rambling theory, but it was real clear that that was how I was letting myself know I was here, by God, and that I needed to be here. And when I started doing it the pain started going away. I learned in doing it with others that you *can* give it away.

CP: I can move my pain, too. When it starts to hurt I think about the other knee. I don't actually move the pain, but I concentrate on this and . . . it's not ignoring it, but it's kind of like I let the pain wash around me. I can work with it that way. I tried biofeedback and that didn't work for shit for me. But buying the femur and putting it in the drawer, that was the thing that finally did it.

HS: See, that's almost pure shamanic work.

CP: I've got two good ones now, that's how I look at it. Two good ones.

HS: When you place all of that memory, that traumatic memory, into that femur and bury that sucker, you give away the whole experience. You gleaned from it all you need to learn.

CP: I talked about this with another guy, about the moment when he thought he was dying, and he said it hurt him. When I thought I was dying . . . I guess I really was, I thought, "Man, I did everything I can do, there's not another thing I can do to save my life right now." And that was a moment of total peace. The only one I ever had. Total peace.

HS: When I kept going out in that tunnel in that real strong one, the other part was that I was very conscious, even though I was in a coma, of a lot of shit that was going on in the hospital. Weird, vivid memories. I didn't have enough guts until about two years later when I ran into one of the nurses that was on the ward, I said, "I've got something I've gotta ask you. While I was in the coma . . ." and I shared three or four experiences, and she was just stunned. She said, "You couldn't have known that, you were in total coma." But I did. See, there's another part of us functioning—that's no theory on my part, I *know* that—that is watching this whole frigging thing happen. It's that part that I think is really our source of power. It's there that you pull through.

I saw a guy get hit in the thigh. Wasn't even as bad as the thigh wound I got. We had the sulfa packs on him, I mean, he was treated fast. He died in five minutes. Five fucking minutes and the dude checks out. And then there was another guy that got hit in the guts, and for seventy-two hours, because we were in constant fire, he was literally at one point, and boy, this is a horrible image in my mind, stuffing his intestines back in his frigging body. All of us thought it was goodbye time. He kept saying, "Don't fucking look at me like that, I'm not dying." And the sonofabitch didn't die. You can't live through that kind of shit, man, and not understand that you choose your death on some level. The one guy, five minutes, and it wasn't even a serious wound. Wasn't even bleeding that bad. There's something going on there. It's one of the big mysteries in life, I think. But I definitely think you choose your death.

CP: I remember having the option of going crazy or not. I could just let myself go and go that way. I've gotten that from accident victims, too, guys who've been really broken up in car wrecks, who've said they consciously pulled back from that.

HS: Yeah, I think I'll take this step over here into the twilight zone for a while.

CP: I had no idea that it was a temporary possibility. To me it was an all-out choice, either I'm going to go crazy or I'm not. I was in the hospital at the time. I never thought I could just walk over there for a little while and take a look around and come home.

HS: A lot of people don't know that. That's something I learned from working with a guy named Marty Lane. He just passed away recently, but he was probably one of the best with schizophrenics. He taught me how to literally go in—he was a psychiatrist, a medical doctor, but he was a shaman, he wasn't a fucking psychiatrist—he showed me how to go in where schizophrenics and catatonics are at. Go right in the same place with them and come right back out. I've gone crazy a few times. I know how to go there and come back, and that's important. Socrates said, "Those who the gods would make gods they first drive insane." (laughs)

That's an important revelation, that there is a moment you face, knowing you can just step into that twilight zone. That you've got that choice. Some choose to do it and come back, some choose to do it and don't come back, and some just say I don't think I'm going to go there.

CP: Part of the reason I didn't go was that I didn't think I needed another problem. Don't need any more challenges right now. (laughs)

HS: Wise choice. The third hit, because I jumped from two to four, that's probably the weirdest one because I know the least about it. We'd gone in on what you call a "lurp," long-range reconnaissance patrol, with a HALO (High-Altitude Low-Opening parachute) unit. There were only about four HALO units that really worked hard in 'Nam. Stupidly, I was in one of 'em. This was way up in Cambodia/Laos, so if anything happens up there, it doesn't happen. I always found that most peculiar, that something could happen and not happen. I believe that's why this one just . . . but it's the one where I came out with so much shrapnel in my back. We went in with seventeen men and four of us came back. We were out there sixteen days. I got hit several times, and one, particularly, was running. I was running so fast that I literally couldn't feel the ground under my feet. Out of fear. I know it sounds stupid, but I swear to God I was running across the top of those rice paddies. I was haulin' ass, Jack. I remember the sound, I can remember the sound of the explosion and seeing my body catapulting through the air, and the next thing I know I was still running. What happened at that point, I haven't the foggiest fuckin' idea. I was still haulin' ass. I got on the chopper and got three more guys . . . and we were out and away. I have absolutely no memory of anything. I didn't have any pain. None whatsoever.

When we lifted off and I knew we were okay, and . . . even the Huey got hit. It didn't go down but it smoked all the way back. I was laughing, talking, it was the most dissociated experience I've ever had. There was no pain on that one, none whatsoever. When I got in the hospital and they showed me a needle I passed out 'cause I hate needles. (laughs) I got a fucking fear of needles that won't quit. The nurse came in and said, "Well we'll take care of it," and I saw the needle and went, "Check out time," boom. (laughs) Next thing I knew I woke up in the recovery unit. They'd taken out what shrapnel they could, and what they couldn't, they couldn't.

The only thing I can add to that is in Dallas, Texas—that hit happened in '65—I was teaching a workshop, I always sit cross-legged, and I was teaching a workshop and I reached across for an ashtray and pain on this right nerve plexus goes all the way down this arm, hit me worse than any pain I've ever experienced. Including all the stuff I've been sharing with you. I couldn't move. I mean I could not move. To make a long story short, a thumbnail-sized piece of shrapnel, it showed up on the X-ray, had shifted up into a nerve. That stuff gravitates, it moves. It hit the inside of the nerve plexus. Still, I've got numbness in the right thumb and right fingers. Boy. They said they could operate but if they did there was a 50 percent chance I'd lose my whole right arm and I said, "Fuck you. Forget it."

I've been doing deep tissue massage, and only about two months ago did I finally slip out of the pain state. So it lasted about a year and a half . . . yeah, because I'll be going back to Dallas in December so it's almost two years. Except for the last three months I was in *constant* pain. It just would not go away. Doing my martial arts, doing everything, I just learned to moderate it, to put the pain away, go into it and forget about it.

But see, that's really the direct result of that experience where I had no pain during the whole thing. It was almost like a comedy. The only thing I remember is how great it felt to be able to run so goddamn fast. That's when I really felt like a swift deer, because I was haulin' ass. This was probably a ten- or fifteen-minute run. We were at the edge of the jungle and the Huey was coming down and we had to break across the open field in order to get to it. They were right on our asses. And boy, it was really interesting. I have never, ever, run like that.

All that experience, all the shrapnel, it was like Disneyland. All I wanted was freedom, and that was freedom. That was my focus. All this back here was like, no way. Don't deal with that. I think that was when I learned about implied intent. I had one fucking intent and nothing was gonna keep me from getting there. They said there was something like twenty-odd pieces of shrapnel in me and they dug out all but six pieces. They were in too deep and they said, "Well, they'll move around some but they won't bother you." They didn't until . . . and then, *whoa*! Interestingly enough, we used magnets. A guy down there in Texas uses electromagnetic therapy, and that helped a lot, and using deep tissue massage to move it away and get rid of the scar tissue around the nerve plexus. Of course that hurts, you know, the treatment's almost as bad as the pain, except that after the treatment you feel great. It's like somebody turned a knob. . . . Each treatment the pain gets a little less, and now I've been out of pain for about two months.

Well, that's all my stories. . . .

CP: You've got one, you said you were a Texas Ranger.

HS: Highway patrolman. That one's kind of stupid. I got

one right here, a .22 (laughs) went through the wrist and came out right there, see where it's white? You wanna talk about knife scars, I got a bunch of those fuckers. This really sounds stupid, but I'd rather get shot than cut. Cuts . . . if a guy pulls a knife on me I get real crazy. Something happens that's real strange. It's a craziness but a calmness at the same time. I *know* I'm gonna get cut, that's the first thing I learned. Just accept that you're gonna get cut. I dislike knives tremendously.

This [cut] was pretty bad, you can see, it starts over here and comes across and looks like a snake. The other one comes all the way across this thumb, that one was a straight razor held backhand. As he swung I was getting ready to block and saw it coming and went right straight across and he just . . . that one opened it up so I could see the bone wiggling around inside. I don't like that shit. That makes me nervous. (laughs) I don't like to shed my own blood. That bothers me almost as bad as needles.

This [gunshot], this was a kid. Robbed a liquor store, sixteen years old. We caught him coming out the back door and running down the alley and I yelled at him to halt and I fired in the air. He turned and I saw it was a .22. I had my piece in my right hand, and I started moving sideways to hit my buddy and knock him out of the way, and caught the round in the wrist. There was a real burning, searing pain, again, but it was about the least of all the experiences. I fired and hit him right square in the chest. Pure instinct.

*****

They told me I was going to limp for the rest of my life, and seven months after they told me that I won the United States ju jutsu championship, so fuck them and the horse they rode in on. I don't like medical doctors and I don't like their goddamn opinions about my body. At all. You can hear the anger [in my voice]. I don't fucking trust those people, I don't like them, and I will not ever go in the hospital. Diane knows, if I ever have a cardiac arrest or something, fucking leave me lay there and die. Don't you put my ass in the hospital. If it's my time to die, I'll die. You let me do it my way, with dignity and integrity as a warrior. Don't put me in the hospital. I do not like those places.

Shaman, teacher, wise man, Dr. Swiftdeer lives in the Los Angeles area.

■ PRESTON TOWNES

It was in a bar in El Paso, I worked there as a bouncer. This was back in 1971. There were two guys and they were drunk and obnoxious and I had to throw them out. I'd been doing this for a little while, and I wasn't a hothead kid or anything, you know. I always tried to avoid problems, avoid conflict. They were not paying me to beat up on people and throw them in the street; they were paying me to remove people who were a liability to the establishment or who were molesting the other patrons. These two were doing both.

I'd given them one warning earlier, and I'd told them that this was going to be their last drink. They were cut off. This was before the days of the liquor liability law, but the same concept was employed there, you understand what I'm saying? It was a pretty big bar, it was called The Barn. We'd had some trouble with underage girls getting in there and so on. Some scooter trash would hang out there on occasion, but I wouldn't call it a full-on biker bar. You know, I guess you would say it was a cross between a cowboy and a biker bar. This was the early seventies, the hippies had sort of faded out but there was still some hippieism going on.

With my associate, we . . . they demanded to be served, and I'd told them I'd cut them off, and we had to pick 'em up and drag 'em out. They're not real big, they were really about my size. One of them was a little heavier, probably just from drinking so much.

I'm talking to him the whole time I'm bringing him out

to the front of the bar. The technique is to never let them re-cover their balance and keep them moving. I don't know if you're familiar with aikido concepts like that, but as long as you keep a person's balance just a half-step ahead of him, he has to keep going for that half step and can't do much else in the meantime. He can't draw a weapon, he can't do any-thing really. If he tries to do anything else but keep catching his balance, and it's not a dramatic thing, then he will lose his balance. So his posture sense won't allow him to do that.

But when you get him to a door, that's the deal. I got him to the door and gave him a slight push out. So now he's out of the premises, and I said, "You're out of here, don't try to come back or we'll call the fucking police on you."

Then he steps forward, and I'm always very alert for hands, you know, reaching, because the only way you can deploy a weapon is through hand motion and through the use of hands. With a few exotic exceptions. So his hand goes into his coat and I know he's coming up with something but I don't know what it is for sure. So I trap his wrist inside his jacket with my left hand and I hear the shot. The shot goes off with the gun still underneath his leather jacket. The bul-let goes through his leather jacket, the gun was pointed at a downward angle apparently, and strikes me in the shin. Right in the center of the shin, too. It was a .22 Short, so by the time it had gone through his leather jacket and then hit me in the shin, it had lost a lot of its juice. So it didn't break my leg, didn't break the bone in my leg, and the bullet actu-ally didn't stay inside my skin, it bounced out.

I wasn't aware at that instant that I really had been shot, you know, I didn't really think about anything. I heard the gunshot but of course it was muffled under his coat. I pulled his fucking hand out and saw the gun in his hand—this is all one motion—I snatched the gun out of his hand, I turn, strike, and brought the gun down hard on the side of his face.

That pretty much had the desired effect. His buddy ran off across the highway there, whatever highway it was. Well, I was very cross with this person (laughs) so I stomped him a little bit to make sure that he couldn't get up for a while. By then the other two bouncers were on him, holding him, and I still had his gun in my hand. It was a Beretta Minx. I still have the gun in my gun cabinet.

Then I looked at my leg and saw it was bleeding and felt around and said, "Well shit, there can't be a bullet inside here, can there?" Because my leg's not broken and I'm bleeding, and I can see the bone, the white bone because there's not much meat on the shin. By this time the whole fucking leg starts throbbing, and I said, "Oh shit." And I didn't find the bullet, so I assume it bounced out.

Then the police came. It was dark outside the bar, and now it was a big deal with police cars and all this shit. And I pretended that we couldn't find the gun, and I hid it and came back for it later. I don't know why exactly. I didn't want to give it to the cops. And I already had it. It was mine now. (laughs) I still have it.

But you know what happened, when I hit him in the head with it, the magazine must have fallen out and some cop must have found the magazine. Because when I went back to where I'd stashed it, the magazine wasn't in the gun. And I had that gun for several years, seven or eight years, before I happened to find a magazine for it at a gun show.

I never gave him a chance to truly deploy the weapon. My guess is, it's an external-hammer, single-action automatic pistol, so that means he had to have a round chambered and the hammer down on a live chamber. He would have had to thumb back the hammer for the first shot. I think what may have happened is that when I grabbed his wrist he was just in the act of thumbing it back. This is supposition. But he only fired one shot, that much is established. And the bullet did go through his clothing, through the inside of his jacket on the left side, exited his leather and hit me. It made a hole in my pants leg that didn't seem large enough for a bullet to go through. I still have a mark on my leg from it, I'm looking at it right now, matter of fact. You can definitely see it.

There's definitely a depression there. Some missing tissue.
But I have no problems from it.

Preston Townes was interviewed by telephone from his home
in the mountains.

▪ ABOUT THE AUTHOR

A native of Southern California, Chris Pfouts has lived all over the United States. He has worked as a mechanic, armed guard, bartender, assistant funeral director, truck driver, writer, and editor. Pfouts has a degree in journalism from New York University and belongs to Kappa Tau Alpha, the journalism honor society. A lifelong biker, Pfouts has edited *Iron Horse*, a biker magazine, for four years. He now edits *Classic Cycle Review*. His writing has also appeared in *SPIN, OUI, New Choices, Easyriders, Outlaw Biker, American Motorcyclist*, the *New York Daily News Sunday Magazine, Tattoo Advocate, Tattoo Revue*, and other publications. Among his many hobbies Pfouts includes collecting books and records, studying New Orleans history, drinking beer, and traveling.